PRAISE FOR

Harvard Schmarvard

"This book gives us a welcome and helpful way of looking at college and university rankings. Jay Mathews offers refreshing insights into the college admissions process and makes the important point that getting into the 'best' college is less important than choosing the college that *brings out the best* in every student."

—Richard W. Riley, former U.S. Secretary of Education

"In a day when college-bound students are inundated with recruitment material and confusing claims of merit, Jay Mathews provides important guidance to help families navigate the college selection and application process."

—William J. Bennett, former U.S. Secretary of Education

"*Harvard Schmarvard* is a smart, contrarian perspective on the pressure-filled college admissions process, by one of the country's best education writers. It's combination of advice, research, wit, and first-person tales from the front-lines deserves to be read by every high school student and every parent."

—David A. Kaplan, senior editor, *Newsweek*

"There may be a better book on college admissions than Mathews', but I don't know what it is. Among overanxious candidates and parents—including me—nothing is more important than demolishing the silly idea that not getting into Harvard (or Duke, Stanford, or some other 'prestige' school) is a life-ending experience. Mathews does this and provides an immense amount of useful information about tests, guidance counselors, college selection, and early admissions. The book has the added advantage of being compulsively readable."

—Robert J. Samuelson, *Newsweek* columnist

"Jay Mathews gets it. He puts into perspective what has become an increasingly out-of-control college admissions process. Any family embarking on this path will benefit from this guide."

—Seppy Basili, coauthor, *The Unofficial, Biased Guide to the 320 Most Interesting Colleges*

"This book will free teens and parents from that stupid myth that college quality is measured by selectivity or name. A badly needed public service that lays bare the rankings fraud and the complicity of colleges in it."

—Loren Pope, author, *Colleges That Change Lives*

"It would be great if all college-bound students read this book; for their parents, it should be mandatory. I don't agree with every tip that Jay Matthews offers, but on the whole his is a wonderful voice of sanity on a subject that has driven much of America nuts."

—James Fallows, *The Atlantic Monthly*

"*Harvard Schmarvard* demystifies and demythologizes the college selection process. Jay Mathews gives high school seniors and their parents a fresh and challenging perspective to college admissions that flies in the face of 'street wisdom' and the college rating guides."

—Greg Feldmeth, assistant headmaster, Polytechnic School

"Finally, a resouce for *all* college-bound students, not just the elite. Mathews' style is straightforward and honest. He provides realistic advice in a down-to-earth, humorous style. I will encourage all of my students and their parents to read this book."

—Sally C. O'Rourke, high school counselor

"Selecting a college is one of the most important decisions many families make. Mathews both entertains and educates in making that decision a better one and, most importantly, making it one that both parents and students will be happy with. Calmly, clearly, with humor and zest, Mathews provides practical and jargon-free advice on how students can get the best education for *them*."

—Dick Reed, Fairfax County, Virginia, parent

JAY MATHEWS

HARVARD SCHMARVARD

GETTING BEYOND THE
IVY LEAGUE TO THE COLLEGE
THAT IS BEST FOR YOU

PRIMA PUBLISHING

Published by Prima Publishing, Roseville, California. Member of the Crown Publishing Group, a division of Random House, Inc., New York.

PRIMA PUBLISHING and colophon are trademarks of Random House, Inc., registered with the United States Patent and Trademark Office.

Library of Congress Cataloging-in-Publication Data
Mathews, Jay.
  Harvard schmarvard : getting beyond the Ivy League to the college that is best for you / Jay Mathews.—1st ed.
      p.   cm.
  Includes index.
  ISBN 0-7615-3695-7
  1. Universities and colleges—United States—Admission.   I. Title.
LB2351.2 .M25   2002
378.1'61'0973—dc21   2002153154

03 04 05 06 07 TT 10 9 8 7 6 5 4 3 2 1
Printed in the United States of America

First Edition

Visit us online at www.primapublishing.com

To Linda, Joe, Peter, and especially Katie,
who handled applying to college better than I did

CONTENTS

INTRODUCTION

*I*N THE LAST 20 years I have interviewed hundreds of high school students, as well as their teachers and parents, about the frustrations and disappointments of applying to college. Those conversations have convinced me that most American families do not truly understand what is important in finding the best school.

In this book, I will share the stories of many parents and students who have stumbled through the process. But let's start with a particularly sad case: me. When I was in my late teens, through my own lack of foresight, I had the rare experience of attending two very different colleges. I saw firsthand how wrong many of the myths are about what makes a good undergraduate experience.

Like most people, my parents and I began our search for a school without a clear idea of what I *really* wanted or a deep appreciation of what the available colleges offered. The result was that I first went to Occidental College in Los Angeles, then, as now, a very fine school. When it did not give me everything that I wanted, I transferred to Harvard University in Cambridge, Massachusetts, and found that famous place also lacking in many respects.

I chose Occidental because I had visions of becoming the U.S. ambassador to China. I dreamed of single-handedly establishing a new era of amity between America and the People's Republic. Oxy, as it is called, had a highly praised diplomacy and world affairs department. I also liked its vibrant political atmosphere. During my freshman year there were passionate debates between supporters of President Lyndon Baines Johnson and his Republican challenger, Barry Goldwater. Most of the professors were excellent. The western civilization course gave me the deepest and most engaging academic experience I had ever had.

But the diplomacy and world affairs department, the most important factor in my choice, was a disappointment. The chairman of the department proved to be an unimaginative teacher and an uninspiring person. The first week I was there, he told me and several other freshmen that we would never succeed as Foreign Service Officers because we had failed to respond formally to his invitation to an afternoon tea at his house.

I transferred to Harvard because I was, like many of my generation, in love with the image of President Kennedy and resolved to carry on his political legacy after his assassination. He had been a government major at Harvard, so I became one too. Then I discovered that the courses at America's oldest university were not nearly as well taught as the political science classes at much younger and lesser-known Occidental. Harvard's government courses were full of contradictory theories that gave me a headache.

Why didn't I leave and try my luck with school number three? I might have if I had not found Harvard's student newspaper—which no one told me about before I arrived—and realized it could help me learn a trade that could, and eventually did, get me to Beijing.

The more people I interview about the connection between their college choices and their subsequent lives, the more I realize that no decision about where to go to school is ever going to be perfect. But that fact is almost never mentioned by the college guides and guidance counselors and admissions officers and university Web sites and other popular sources of information about this process.

So repeat after me: Whatever college I choose, there is going to be something wrong with it—and that is okay.

Some people say picking a college is as serious and vital a decision as choosing a spouse. According to this line of thought, if you do it right, a life of pleasure and satisfaction awaits you. Mess it up, and you will feel a great deal of pain and regret, even if you find a way to end the relationship.

I believe that way of thinking is wrong. Choosing a college is much more like buying a house. It is a major investment, but only those few people obsessed with real estate expect their choice of residence to change their life. If it turns out the bedrooms are not big enough, or the living room is too hot in the summer, it is relatively easy to make another choice. The long-term emotional and financial damage is usually minimal.

Your friends may tell you being admitted to a college with a luminous name will guarantee a life of happiness, but all the available evidence suggests they are wrong. Getting into a brand-name school like Yale, Stanford, or Amherst will not alter your occupational, financial, and romantic future any more than buying that nice French colonial on Elm Street. As we shall see, the notion that the brand-name schools can guarantee high salaries and satisfying careers for all their graduates is a scam. The success of many graduates of Ivy League schools is a matter of qualities established long before they ever got to college and has little, if anything, to do with what they learned or whom they met at those great universities.

Young people who possess the habits and instincts that lead to productive lives, students with persistence, honesty, charm, and common sense, are heavily represented in the ranks of those admitted to well-known schools. But other students with the same character traits—formed long before they took take an SAT test—often go to schools their grandmothers have never heard of and do just as well in their occupations. In many cases they get even more credit for their success because no one can say they had to rely on their old school connections. (Which is another myth. Everybody has useful connections, if they exert themselves to use them. It is the effort—that strength of character again—and not the connection that makes the difference.)

So relax. Picking a school is at least as much fun as picking a house and should be handled with the same clear-eyed assessment of each possibility's assets and drawbacks.

Enjoy the campus tours. Fantasize about your future. Weigh all the factors. But remember each school is just a collection of buildings and people. You cannot know how it will work out for you until you live with it for a while. You will find it has unforeseen flaws, but what doesn't? You can choose to live with it, or, like me, try another school. Either way, it is your heart and soul that will make your fortune, not the size of the college's endowment or whether it was founded before the Revolutionary War.

Now, let's examine, one by one, your worries, hopes, and fears about selecting a college so that you can survive the process with not only your self-esteem and optimism intact, but with your family members still speaking to each other and your view of your future (and your children's) still bright.

Harvard Schmarvard

THE DUST CLEARS

What Really Matters About Choosing a College

Whatever the impact on your life, choosing a college is a serious business. It is a decision important to you or, if you're a parent, your son or daughter. If that weren't so, you most likely would not be reading this book. So let's take a moment and exercise your imagination: High school is almost over and college is looming on the horizon. Those college acceptance and rejection letters are on the way or are about to pop up on your e-mail list. You are worried that you or your child is not going to get into the "right" college, which probably means a college with a big name. Try playing this game, which I call "Which college is hardest to get into?"

Easy question, right? Harvard, you say. Nope. Georgetown? A fine school, but not the most selective. Princeton? Close, but wrong again.

Perhaps you think this is a silly pastime. Who cares which school accepts the lowest percentage of applicants? There are plenty of good colleges. The one that best suits a student's needs is the one to attend, you say, no matter how hard or easy it is to get into.

You are right, of course. That is the healthy and sensible attitude. Yet deep in the hearts of many applicants and their parents is the nagging feeling that the best schools are the famous ones most likely to reject them, and going to a lesser-known school means they are in some way inadequate. People denied entry to the hottest new dance clubs feel the same way.

> Deep in the hearts of many applicants and their parents is the nagging feeling that the best schools are the famous ones most likely to reject them.

This belief is based on the assumption that the choosiest schools are the brand-name universities whose graduates include Nobel laureates, Supreme Court justices, and big winners on *Jeopardy.* But what if that were not entirely true? Applicants and their families might then be able to toss the Ivy U rejection letter into the trash with a shrug and a smile.

Thus our game. Which college is hardest to get into? This changes from year to year, so there is more than one answer—and that answer is almost always a surprise.

THE SURPRISING TRUTH ABOUT "SELECTIVE" COLLEGES

LET US TAKE a recent year, 2000. Here is the answer to the quiz: The most selective college in the country that year, accepting only 9.6 percent of its applicants was . . . drum roll please, and in this case a toot on the boatswain's pipe . . . the U.S. Coast Guard Academy. According to the Kaplan-*Newsweek How to Get Into College* guide, the nation's most selective school was composed of one thousand young saltwater fanatics on a New London, Connecticut, campus full of ropes and charts and faculty members who have made their reputations busting drug runners.

Captain Robert W. Thorne, the director of admissions at the academy that year, was pleased with his school's number 1 status. The academy's free tuition and room and board were a major draw, he said, but the students knew how hard it was to get in, and that added to the esprit de corps.

College acceptance rates are full of surprises. Some of the big brand names did appear on the Kaplan-*Newsweek* list for 2000. Harvard, with an 11.4 percent acceptance rate, was number 3. Princeton was number 4; Columbia, number 6; Stanford, number 8; Yale, number 10; Amherst, number 14; and Georgetown, with a 22.8 percent rate, number 20.

But also on the list were the military academies and three schools most Americans have never heard of: Cooper Union (number 5), a tuition-free art, architecture, and engineering school in Manhattan; Talladega College (number 18), a historically black liberal arts school near Birmingham, Alabama; and the Mason Gross School of the Arts (number 19), part of Rutgers University. On the 2002 list, Julliard and the College of the Ozarks made appearances.

Brand-name identification and exclusivity among colleges may not be as closely related as most Americans assume. Many Americans will be surprised to learn it was harder to get into Middlebury College (26 percent acceptance rate) in Vermont than the University of Virginia (34 percent). Claremont McKenna College, a small school in the smoggy eastern edges of Los Angeles County, was more selective (28 percent) than Ivy League member Cornell (33 percent). And Wellesley, a mecca for ambitious young women, alma mater of Senator Hillary Rodham Clinton and former secretary of state Madeline K. Albright, had a higher acceptance rate (46 percent) than two California schools, Pepperdine (35 percent) and the University of Southern California (USC; 37 percent), long thought to be open to any young person with a tuition check and a craving for surfing, football, or parties.

Some will quibble that entry standards differ. The average SAT scores of the young women applying to Wellesley, for instance, are higher than the average for the Pepperdine applicant pool. But such comparisons mean little to you and your children. The most important thing for your happiness is how difficult it is to get into the school you desire, not some place on some other student's list.

During the years that I have spent writing about colleges and education, I have received a wealth of interesting letters and stories. I could summarize what people have shared with me, but I think it is most illuminating simply to let you hear their words. Throughout this book I will share the stories of others' college experiences in the hopes that they will help you clarify your own needs.

> Brand-name identification and exclusivity among colleges may not be as closely related as most Americans assume.

So, a word to those lucky few who are crossing San Pasqual Street in a new CalTech sweatshirt, or sipping a milkshake at the Peninsula Fountain and Grill near Stanford, or catching a band at Toad's Place just off the Yale campus: You are to be congratulated for being admitted to such fine schools. But since you are not being soaked to the skin as you ride a stormy wave on the U.S. Coast Guard three-masted barque Eagle, you have not, for what it's worth, reached the most selective collegiate environment. And as you will learn in the pages ahead, that is far from being the most important factor in choosing the college that is right for you.

THE REAL PAYOFF: WHAT ARE THE BENEFITS OF THAT BRAND-NAME COLLEGE?

IN THE SUMMER of 1998, Stacy Berg Dale, a short, auburn-haired, and very curious twenty-nine-year-old, sat in her office on the second floor of the Andrew W. Mellon Foundation Research Center, an old white frame house with green trim in a residential

NEUROTIC LIGHTWEIGHTS ARE EVERYWHERE!

The oft-asked question: Will my future be toast if I don't go to an Ivy League school? A good friend of mine is, like me, a land-grant woman with an Ivy League husband. For years we have observed the truth of your story among our mutual friends: An Ivy League education gives you valuable contacts and an impressive resume, but after that you're on your own. You can't wear your school on your forehead. (Okay, some people do, but I don't invite them to dinner.) Among our acquaintances there are as many state school types as Ivy Leaguers who are sophisticated, happy high achievers. Both groups seem to have their share of small-bore, neurotic lightweights as well.

—LINDA KNAUSS

section of Princeton, New Jersey. Reports, books, and printouts rose in untidy stacks all around her as she fiddled with the numbers on her computer screen.

Dale was employed by Mellon to dig into one of the mother lodes of educational research, the College and Beyond Survey of seventy-five thousand students who enrolled in thirty-four colleges in the years 1951, 1976, and 1989. The survey had been compiled for a much-delayed study of college athletics but also had been mined by researchers seeking clues about the impact of selective colleges on particular kinds of students, especially minorities.

Dale was absorbed with the 23,572 students who had entered college in 1976, and in particular with the 70 to 80 percent of that group who had responded to a mail and telephone survey conducted for Mellon by Mathematica Policy Research, Inc., from 1995 to 1997. The survey had asked, among other things, where else they had applied in 1976 and how much money they were making some twenty years later.

Dale had attended a well-regarded public high school in the Chicago suburbs, Oak Park and River Forest High in Oak Park, Illinois. She had been rejected by an Ivy League school, Harvard, but hadn't felt much pain because she had wanted to go to Michigan. She even rejected Rice, as selective as many of the Ivies, to matriculate at Ann Arbor.

She didn't look it, wearing sweater, slacks, and glasses and peering at the computer screen, but Dale had been a heavily recruited athlete. On the tennis court, the giggly teenager became a hitting machine, putting top-spin drives so consistently into the farthest corners that opponents disintegrated in frustration and fatigue. She received a four-year scholarship and was Michigan's top female singles player before graduating in 1991 and moving east.

She gravitated to social and economics issues. As a research associate, she participated in the massive crunching of the Mellon data that yielded the 1998 book *The Shape of the River: Long Term Consequences of Considering Race in College and University Admissions* by former Princeton University president William G. Bowen and former Harvard University president Derek Bok. That study reported that minorities admitted to selective colleges, despite having average test scores lower than their white classmates, did well in college and earned high salaries later on. Elite higher education seemed to give them an advantage, but Dale wondered whether that was true for everyone admitted to Bowen's and Bok's fine schools.

She had known students at Ann Arbor who, like her, had chosen Michigan over more selective universities. She wondered how that affected their lives. So she tried something that no other Mellon researcher had done. She looked at students who had been accepted by the most selective colleges but attended less choosy schools, and then she compared their salaries years later with those of similar students who had gone to the most elite institutions.

REAL KEYS TO SUCCESS

Four years ago I graduated from Robinson High School in Fairfax County, Virginia, as a valedictorian with high SAT scores and what I believed to be very good credentials. I was wait-listed at Harvard and some other Ivy League schools, was accepted at Duke, and was an Echols scholar at the University of Virginia.

I decided to go to Virginia Commonwealth University because of the financial benefits (they offered me a full merit scholarship for all four years) and also because I thought they had excellent resources to pursue my desire to go to medical school. After finishing the medical school application process this year, I will be attending Stanford medical school in the fall.

It was definitely not the reputation of my school that carried me to this position, but my hard work, persistence, and ambition. I hope that all college-bound students learn that there are plenty of good educational opportunities everywhere, and you don't have to go to an institution with a stellar academic reputation to reach your goals. One only needs to have the motivation, dedication, and ambition to succeed.

—DAN CHAO

Most of the research to that point said that a nicely printed diploma from a New England college at least three centuries old was worth major dollars later in life. Harvard economist Caroline Hoxby, for instance, concluded that "men who graduate from more selective colleges tend to earn substantially more by age 32 than men who graduate from less selective colleges." The lifetime difference between a man who had entered a top-ranked college and one who had entered a school on the bottom rank of her wide-ranging scale in 1982 was more than $1.15 million.

> Stacy Dale found no significant difference in income between those who had gone to elite schools and those who had been accepted at those schools but had chosen to go elsewhere.

But that's not what Stacy Dale concluded. She found no significant difference in income between those who had gone to elite schools and those who had been accepted at those schools but had chosen to go elsewhere. She found some indications that even students who had applied and been rejected by very selective colleges were doing just as well twenty years later as those who had gotten in.

Unknown in the field, without a Ph.D., she was not going to challenge the prevailing opinion on her own. She might be reading the data incorrectly or repeating work that had already been done. She went looking for help.

FROM OCCIDENTAL COLLEGE TO HARVARD UNIVERSITY

MY OWN FRESHMAN year was spent at Occidental College in Eagle Rock, California. Its 1,500 students were tucked away on a tree-lined campus often used for movie and television scenes, in a faded Los Angeles suburb full of tidy little stucco homes. For my sophomore year I transferred to Harvard, a college four times as big and infinitely more famous. I graduated in 1967.

My parents had attended Long Beach City College. My father had taken a few courses at USC but never got a degree. My mother graduated from UCLA, which seemed to her more than good enough for anyone. She wasn't happy about my going to Harvard, but she let me do it, working full-time as a teacher to help pay for it.

My initial disillusionment with Harvard faded a bit when I discovered the student newspaper. I fell in love with the managing editor. I learned reporting skills that allowed me to get a job. But as a journalist I have met many people smarter and richer than I am who attended colleges I have never heard of. The more I thought about the mystique of universities like Harvard, the more I wondered—as did Stacy Dale—whether they deserved their reputations for ensuring good lives.

CHARACTER? OR THE COLLEGE YOU CHOOSE?

ALAN B. KRUEGER, Bendheim professor of economics and public policy at Princeton and director of the Survey Research Center at the Woodrow Wilson School, was an academic star and not yet forty. Former Princeton president Bowen, now president of the Mellon Foundation, asked him to help Stacy Dale investigate her interesting research findings. He drove over to the Mellon Center to talk to her.

The tall, lean Krueger had grown up in Livingston, New Jersey. He had been an excellent student and track star with a fifty-four-second time in the quarter mile and a six-foot-high jump. He had no trouble getting into his first-choice school, Cornell. He quickly discarded law school plans and gravitated to economics, where there was a chance of contributing something new rather than replowing old precedents.

Perched on a chair in Dale's cluttered office, Krueger found he shared a number of interests with her. They both were fascinated by the Mellon database. They both wondered whether success depended more on a student's character than a college's name. And they both played tennis, although once they took to the court, Krueger was awed to discover she always won.

They prepared a paper for a meeting of the National Bureau of Economic Research titled "Estimating the Payoff to Attending a More Selective College: An Application of Selection on Observables and Unobservables." There were some dense sentences: "Without loss of generality, assume that X1 and X2 are scalar variable." But their point was clear.

Dale and Krueger agreed that graduates of more selective schools on average did have higher incomes than graduates of less selective ones. But this had little to do with the choosiness of the schools, they argued. The most important reason graduates of the Harvards, Yales, and Princetons had bigger salaries later in life was not because they had so many talented classmates at their selective alma maters but because of personal characteristics they brought with them to college—habits and tendencies that had developed long before they started calculating their grade-point averages.

> The most important reason graduates of the Harvards, Yales, and Princetons had bigger salaries later in life was not because they had so many talented classmates at their selective alma maters but because of personal characteristics they brought with them to college.

The two researchers studied 14,239 students at thirty colleges, ranging from the most selective, including Yale and Swarthmore, to much less picky schools like Denison and Penn State. They noted which schools had accepted and rejected which students, and they compared their subsequent earnings.

Then they devised a strategy to implicitly adjust for students' crucial "unobserved characteristics," such as persistence, humor, and warmth, that might have influenced success, both in the admissions game and in life. To do this, they grouped together students who had been accepted and rejected by similar colleges. Admissions officers apparently saw the same qualities in them, yet some in each group eventually attended very selective schools, and some did not. The researchers concluded, "Students who attended more selective colleges do not earn more than other students who were accepted and rejected by comparable schools but attended less selective colleges."

CHARACTER COUNTS

I was raised in a factory worker's home in the southeast side of Detroit in a not-so-nice neighborhood. Wayne State, a big-city state school, was what I could afford. When I attended the University of Michigan [as a graduate student], I met for the first time graduates from the "exclusive schools." I determined that they were no more or less educated than myself. I am now retired after having a twenty-eight-year career as a planner for the County of San Diego, California. During my work career I met fellow professionals who graduated from the famous and not-so-famous schools. Frankly, I could not tell the difference. Character, hard work, and intelligence were the only differences.

—DAVE LASSALINE

While at Harvard, I learned that many Ivy Leaguers, including me, assumed that we would one day wield great power. But once out in the real world, I've learned that my faith in the triumph of the elite was not well founded. Elite school graduates are no more immune that anyone else to the widening gap between youthful expectations and adult lives. Emotional illness, alcoholism, bad marriages, bad luck, ennui—the red-bound class reports I receive every five years from Harvard are full of accounts of dreams abandoned or severely revised. John Lithgow, the award-winning actor known best for the TV series *3rd Rock from the Sun,* and Tom Ridge, the former Pennsylvania governor and Bush administration homeland security adviser, had both been members of my college class, but so had Alan J. Horowitz, who in his thirty-fifth annual report, sent from a state prison in Fishkill, New York, said his life had been "an uninterrupted saga of frustration, failure and loss."

"SUCCESS" AND THE REAL WORLD

CHARACTER TRAITS, SUCH as persistence, optimism, and honesty, established long before anyone takes the SAT, seemed to me more crucial to success than an Ivy League degree. After all, how much of an advantage has my Ivy diploma been? I got good experience in news writing at Harvard's student newspaper, the *Crimson,* but many *Washington Post* colleagues from less prestigious places, particularly big state universities, have skills I envy. On the day I was hired at the *Post* in 1971, I sat nervously outside the office of executive editor Benjamin C. Bradlee, a Harvard graduate, as he charged past me without a word and scoured the newsroom for people who knew me. I saw him speak briefly to one Harvard graduate reporter and walk off in search of another. I assume they said nice things, because I got the job, but I know Bradlee went through a similar routine for graduates of Maryland and other fine but less self-congratulatory universities.

Perhaps Ivies once ran the *Post* newsroom, but not anymore. Here are the alma maters of the paper's top editors in 2002 in roughly descending order of influence: Ohio State, Occidental, University of Wisconsin–Milwaukee, State University of New York at Buffalo, Colorado State, Harvard, Michigan, American, and Florida. The Occidental alum, managing editor Steve Coll, arrived at that college thirteen years after I left and stayed. He then managed to write four books and win a Pulitzer Prize without having so much as a library card from an Ivy League institution.

Maybe the *Post* is an anomaly, and the link between marquee schools and power thrives elsewhere. But I don't think so. Flip through the *2002 Almanac of American Politics* and note the alma maters of the people we have chosen to lead us. Here are the colleges attended by the first twenty-five governors listed: Alabama, Yale, Kansas, Ouachita Baptist, Stanford, Austin State, Villanova, no college (Delaware governor Ruth Ann Minner is a high school dropout who got her GED), Texas, Georgia, Berkeley, Idaho, Ferris State,

Indiana, Hamilton, Kansas Wesleyan, Kentucky, Louisiana State University, Dartmouth, Florida State, Trinity, Michigan State, North Hennepin Community College (you guessed it—the wrestler), Mississippi, and Southwest Missouri State.

Try the senior U.S. senators of the other twenty-five states, starting in the back of the book and going forward: Wyoming, Wisconsin, Salem, Washington State, Washington & Lee, St. Michael's, Brigham Young University, Georgia, Memphis State, South Dakota State, Clemson, West Point, Penn, Stanford, Oklahoma State, Miami of Ohio, Stanford, Wingate, Harvard, New Mexico, Rutgers, Lafayette, Utah State, Nebraska, and Stanford.

Or how about the colleges of the chief executive officers of the top ten Fortune 500 companies, starting at the top in 2001: Duke, Pittsburg (Kansas) State, Wisconsin, Royal Melbourne Institute of Technology, University of Massachusetts, Dartmouth, Cornell, Miami of Ohio, Institute of Chartered Accountants (Australia), and UC–Berkeley. Some of our most powerful journalists, the network news anchors, went to these institutions: Sam Houston State (Dan Rather) and South Dakota (Tom Brokaw). Peter Jennings, one of the most knowledgeable people in the business, did not go to college. He was so precocious a broadcaster that he dropped out of high school to start his career in his native Canada.

These lists are not nearly as elitist as one would expect if big-name schools ruled. Venture outside the northeastern megalopolis or beyond the pricier parts of the Los Angeles basin and Chicago's North Shore, and you find the number of young people seeking Ivy admission is substantially lower. Many of them, even those with 1,500 SAT scores, are far more interested in attending their home state's best public university.

And those universities, as well as many other lesser-known schools, have gotten much better in the last generation, narrowing the gap between those colleges perceived to be the best and the rest. *Newsweek* and *Washington Post* columnist Robert J. Samuelson, writing in the

2003 edition of the Kaplan-*Newsweek* guide *How to Get Into College,* noted that "in 1967, colleges and universities awarded 558,000 bachelor's degrees. By 2000, the number had roughly doubled to 1.2 million. With larger numbers, many people admitted to 'prestige' schools two or three decades ago would be rejected today. Their modern counterparts attend 'lesser' schools, whose student bodies have almost certainly improved."

Samuelson continued:

The same pressures are operating on college and university faculties. From 1960 to 2000, the annual number of new Ph.D.s rose from 10,575 to almost 45,000. The congestion and capriciousness of college tenure mean that many first-rate scholars settle at schools with lesser nameplates. Consider the Bancroft Prize, awarded to the best scholarly books on U.S. history. Recent winners teach at Amherst and Columbia—and also Boston University and the University of Colorado at Boulder.

THE CHARACTER OF THE STUDENT

IN A MEETING room of the Marriott Hotel in Cambridge in November 1998, Krueger presented the results of their research to several dozen colleagues. Dale sat up front to help with questions. The reaction was positive, but as word of the study spread, some expressed doubts. Dale and Krueger could only compute averages. Individual students might find great benefits in certain schools. Perhaps, some experts suggested, students who went to the Ivies did not gain a financial advantage because they chose less lucrative fields, like teaching. Hoxby, the Harvard economist who had found income advantages in attending higher-ranked colleges, said Dale and Krueger's sample of colleges was too small and did not have a wide enough range of selectivity.

Researchers studying this question acknowledge that later earnings are only one gauge of a college's success. They grant that emotional well-being, commitment to social causes, and job satisfaction can result from a good college experience, but those factors are harder to measure than salary.

Dale, who has since moved to the consulting company Mathematica Policy Research, and Krueger said they looked at data on all colleges by adding a second, nationally representative data set of the class of 1972 and focused on the range most meaningful to middle-class applicants by using the rich College and Beyond data set. They agreed that individual differences were very important. That was their point: Except for low-income students, it was not the choosiness of the school but the character of the student that made the difference. Each person had to find the school that best fit his or her needs.

THE NURTURED NON-IVY STUDENT

If I had read your article in 1991 when I was applying to colleges, I am not sure I would have heeded—or understood—your message, having come from a family that encouraged me to continue the tradition of attending an Ivy League school. Instead, I found myself at Hollins College (Roanoke, Virginia), an enclave of writers, where I earned my B.A. I continued my education at American University in Washington, D.C., where I obtained my M.A., and now find myself in Oklahoma at the University of Tulsa, working on my doctoral dissertation in literature.

I don't feel deprived of a sound education. My professors at Hollins were especially outstanding, committed to nurturing the individual and his or her unique interests.

—PAULINE T. NEWTON

> Except for low-income students, it was not the choosiness of the school but the character of the student that made the difference.

Energetic people would make their mark even if their friends had to ask them to repeat the name of the college they were attending.

Smart students, no matter where they attend college, will use their drive, intelligence, and sense of timing to create a situation where they can succeed, just as Krueger finally did to beat Dale in tennis. He practiced, he strategized, and when Dale, married to an economics professor at Muhlenberg College, was four months pregnant, he lured her back onto the court and won.

HEATHER'S ADVENTURE, PART 1

Heather Dresser does not remember exactly when her mother took charge of her college admissions process. She wasn't paying much attention. The Thomas Jefferson High School for Science and Technology in Fairfax County, Virginia, where she was a student, had a demanding faculty that assigned homework without much thought to her need for sleep. She also had choir, track, and cheerleading practices and horseback riding lessons. College just wasn't on her mind.

Heather's mom, Marcie Dresser, had a degree in early childhood education and had stayed home to raise her children. She was used to getting things organized, so Heather was not surprised to hear that her mother had visited Jefferson's college and career center on her own to do some research. In a preliminary conversation, mother and daughter had decided to look just at schools with Japanese language majors, so she could continue to study the language as she had in high school. This narrowed the pool to about 20 colleges, a manageable group, they thought.

Their first campus visit was to Stanford the summer before Heather's junior year. The family was visiting friends in California, so Heather was persuaded to see the campus while she was there. She was a good student at a very good high school, and no college seemed entirely beyond her reach. She looked at the sprawling adobe campus west of Palo Alto and decided she hated it. There were not enough trees—the palm trees didn't count.

As her junior year began, Heather ignored the college letters and brochures that began to pour in. Her mother filtered them, putting the ones from "good" schools on the bed with the white coverlet in Heather's second-floor bedroom in their home in McLean, Virginia. She would move that mail, without opening or reading it, to the growing stack on the other twin bed in her room that was used for collecting debris.

In the winter of her junior year, still not ready to think about college, Heather agreed to her mother's plea to sit down at their kitchen table and plan her college search. It was clear from their conversation that her parents thought she should seriously consider one of the little brainy schools: Davidson, Amherst, Swarthmore, or the University of Chicago. They thought she was too shy to stand out on a big campus like the University of Michigan.

Heather didn't tell them so, but she knew that she didn't want to stand out. She was more comfortable in a crowd where she could move unnoticed. She wanted to fall through the cracks.

Heather went along with her mother's plan to drive to North Carolina to see Davidson, Duke, and the University of North Carolina at Chapel Hill. But she gave it only minimal attention. She did not start to read the material that her mother had so painstakingly gathered about Davidson until they were in the car, heading south.

We'll come back to Heather's experiences as we proceed through the chapters of this book.

2

RELAX

There's No Such Thing As the Wrong High School

$\mathcal{N}$ OW THAT I have, hopefully, adjusted your attitude a bit, let's explore the process of selecting and applying to the colleges of your choice. It is your junior, or perhaps, your senior year of high school. You have studied hard for the SATs or ACTs, stuffing your mind with exotic vocabulary words and carefully filling in the proper little spaces on the test with a well-sharpened pencil. You have collected all the necessary college application forms and found teachers who will fill out the recommendations. You have cut down on parties and brought up your grades.

So naturally, the experts have come up with a new problem you never considered. Are you already a loser because you picked the wrong high school?

Some educators are warning that eighth grade decisions about which high school to attend may have long-term consequences, including your chances of getting into a selective university. In many communities across the country, students attend high school based on geographic boundaries. In other words, you attend the high school you are zoned for. In an increasing number of places, however, students and their parents can exercise a choice about which regular public high school they attend, or they can choose to attend a charter school or a private school. You may hear a lot about this as you navigate the college admissions process. Let me explain the research and then discuss how much of a problem it is, or is not, for the growing number of students who have a choice of high schools.

HOW HIGH SCHOOL CAN HURT YOU

CITY UNIVERSITY OF New York Graduate Center professor Paul Attewell published the most relevant study in the fall 2001 issue of the journal *Sociology of Education*. The paper is called "The Winner-Take-All High School: Organizational Adaptations to Educational Stratification." It says that, except for a few superstars, attending a very competitive high school hurts your chances of getting into a very selective college.

> Except for a few superstars, attending a very competitive high school hurts your chances of getting into a very selective college.

"Affluent parents, in seeking exceptional high schools to advantage their children, fuel organizational practices that rebound negatively on many of their own children," Attewell said.

He analyzed the scores, courses, class rankings, and high schools of 1,196,213 members of the high school graduating class of 1997 who took College Board tests. For the elite schools, he focused on 217 high schools that had the highest number of graduates with verbal scores of at least 780 on the

SAT. Sixty-seven of them were private schools; 13 were public magnet schools that accept students based on test scores; and 137 were public schools, usually in affluent neighborhoods.

He analyzed the admissions policies of Ivy League schools and noted the importance of class rank, particularly when high school classmates are competing for places at the same selective college. He found that the test scores of students accepted at selective colleges from magnet schools were "substantially higher" than the average for other students admitted to those colleges. He found that, on average, the twenty-ninth-ranked student at a magnet school performed as well on the SAT as the ninth-ranked student in a very strong suburban public school and the top-ranked student in an average high school. Yet the valedictorian at the average school would be rated much higher by most selective colleges than the twenty-ninth-ranked magnet school applicant.

> The valedictorian at the average school would be rated much higher by most selective colleges than the twenty-ninth-ranked magnet school applicant.

So your grade point average at a high-achieving magnet school is likely to be lower than those of your friends back at Neighborhood High, even though your SAT scores are the same. And when you apply to Wedontwant U, the selective university of your dreams—whoops!—you find seventy other kids with 1500 SATs at your magnet school have done the same thing.

Maybe you think this concerns only a few extremely brilliant and privileged students at Andover or St. Albans or New Trier or the Harvard-Westlake School. Yet many parents make important decisions about where they will live and how they will spend their salaries based on which high schools they want for their children. Attewell's paper exposes pecking order values that distort the whole process, including the belief that if you have picked the wrong high school and are not destined for a college a president went to, then you might as well give up and volunteer for the Marines.

HIGH SCHOOL AND YOUR COLLEGE APPLICATION EXPERIENCE

BEFORE WORLD WAR II, this issue had little meaning because young Americans rarely chose their high schools. Except for the very wealthy, teenagers attended the neighborhood school or the parish parochial school, and that was that. Few people went to college, so the connection between secondary and higher education was largely irrelevant.

We are a different country now. About two-thirds of this year's seniors will start college next fall. College defines the American middle class, and the application process is an important rite of passage. My wife and I consider the college nights and campus visits for our daughter to be our last great shared experience, at least until she marries and we get to interfere in her child-rearing decisions. Do the college thing right, and maybe she will call us occasionally after she leaves home. Do it wrong, and we descend to parent hell. So now we not only have to pay attention to college options but also have to worry about the impact of the high school we chose.

There are some very fine neighborhood schools, what Attewell calls "star affluent public schools," which are as good as private schools if you can afford the cost of living in those areas. There are magnet schools, what Attewell calls "star exam public schools," like Lowell in San Francisco, Walnut Hills in Cincinnati, the Illinois Mathematics and Science Academy in Aurora, and Stuyvesant in New York City, which require high scores on an exam to get into. There are demanding private schools, "star prep private schools," such Exeter, St. Louis Country Day, Dalton, Roxbury Latin, Pasadena Polytechnic, and our daughter's school, Sidwell Friends in Washington, D.C.

All of them have a problem when it comes time to compete for college spaces. The students at the magnet program at Montgomery Blair High School in Silver Spring, Maryland, for instance, have an average SAT score of 1480. That is scary enough. But the school also has something called the "4.0/4,000 student," according to Julia Kay, who recently graduated from the Blair magnet program.

I understood the 4.0 part. That's a perfect grade point average. It was the 4,000 part that shook me. It means the student not only has the top SAT-I score of 1,600, but got the top scores of 800 on each of his three SAT-II tests for a grand total of 4,000. At Blair there were two such people in the class of 2002. Although a fine student, Kay said she was keenly aware that she is not one of the two. "I can think of many students in the magnet that would probably be shoo-ins for Ivies if they attended their home high schools," she said, "but in the magnet they just don't stack up."

I visited the most intimidating high school magnet of them all, the Thomas Jefferson High School for Science and Technology in Fairfax County, Virginia. It draws high-performing students from all over northern Virginia. In student achievement, faculty prowess, and sophistication of equipment, no American high school, public

A ROAD LESS TRAVELED

I took an untraditional route for a graduate of the Thomas Jefferson High School for Science and Technology. I went to Mary Washington College, a small liberal arts state school in Fredericksburg, Virginia. I did very well there and now have a great job, which I love. All of my friends from high school are doing well and pursuing their dreams, whether they went to Harvard, Princeton, Notre Dame, William & Mary, UVA, Virginia Tech, or George Mason. Granted, there is prestige that goes along with having a marquee name on a diploma, but hard work and heart will get you a lot further.

—REBECCA EARLE

or private, is quite as good. Yet that means most Jefferson students, when they arrive as ninth graders, realize that for the first time in their lives they are, at least in that context, only average students. Each year several dozen Jefferson seniors with spectacular academic credentials apply to Harvard, Yale, Princeton, Stanford, and other selective schools. Each year 80 percent of them are rejected by those schools, while friends with similar records back at their neighborhood high schools are accepted.

WHAT DO COLLEGES WANT, ANYWAY?

THE COLLEGES ARE reluctant to say it out loud, but they limit the number of students they take from any one high school. Any Ivy League institution could fill its freshman class with just that year's graduates from the top five magnet schools in the country. That class would be no less brilliant than the previous year's admittees from hundreds of high schools. But the guidance counselors of the other high schools suddenly deprived of selective college places would march into the offending university and burn it to the ground. Diversity in admissions means, among other things, a sampling of students from many different high schools, so some students at Jefferson and other competitive high schools are shut out.

> The colleges are reluctant to say it out loud, but they limit the number of students they take from any one high school.

Clarrisse Anderson, a southern California parent, told me her active daughter, who earned a 3.8 grade point average at a top private school, was rejected by her first-choice college, while friends who remained at their local public school graduated at the top of their class and did much better in the college race. "In hindsight, my daughter probably should have gone to the public high school, and she probably would have been valedictorian," Anderson said.

The students in Jennifer Seavey's Advanced Placement (AP) journalism class at Jefferson told me they had some of the same feelings. Tin Nguyen said he wanted to go to Yale, like his brother who graduated from Lee High School in Fairfax, but "I have a much slimmer chance of getting in." Colleges look for awards, but to win one at Jefferson, Greg Polins said, "I have to be better than perfect." Roger Yu said his parents asked why, since he was at Jefferson, he hadn't won a national science prize. Rebecca Weber said the college competition at the school was so frustrating that if she had to do it over, "I would definitely think long and hard before choosing to go to TJ."

This is a typical reaction to the college chase, from both students and parents. How can you win the game if the referee favors your opponent? But the Jefferson students also showed signs of realizing how much of their anxiety is based on nonsense. Weber acknowledged the benefits of "choosing to challenge myself at a rigorous high school." Rachel Schultz said, "We all will be extremely prepared when we get to college, no matter what school it is." Johanna Schaub said being at Jefferson "is an advantage to me and my lifetime pursuit of knowledge."

The American college admission system would have collapsed long ago if bright applicants were actually hurt in any lasting way by not getting into Brown and Amherst. If you don't think so, ask your boss or your mayor or your school superintendent where they went to college. There are at least a hundred American universities whose academic resources are indistinguishable from Harvard's, and the safety schools for graduates of Attewell's star high schools are of a very high order. Every August about a hundred of Jefferson's newest graduates—a quarter of the senior class—get on U.S. Route 29 bound for, appropriately enough, the school founded by Thomas Jefferson himself, the University of Virginia in Charlottesville. "I'm very average as far as TJ kids go," said Kelly Ellis, but "I'm not too worried. UVA loves us."

> There are at least a hundred American universities whose academic resources are indistinguishable from Harvard's.

Attewell says that some high schools twist themselves into unattractive knots to ensure at least some of their students get into the Ivies. His numbers indicate that many students are denied access to AP courses so those at the top of the class will get the necessary attention.

That is bad and should be stopped. If I were looking for a high school appropriate for my child, the first thing I would investigate is how difficult it is to get into college-level courses like AP and International Baccalaureate (IB). You can calculate what I call a Challenge Index rating of the school, using a system I used to prepare Newsweek's list of the nation's Top 100 High Schools.

Take the total number of AP or IB tests given in the most recent year, and divide by the number of seniors graduating that year. If the ratio is 1.000 or higher, and the percentage of tests with scores of 3 or better is no more than 85 percent, then the school is doing a good job opening its courses to many students. You should also look for schools that send more than half their students to four-year colleges and provide significant opportunities for extracurricular activities, particularly the ones that interest your child.

At Jefferson, the Challenge Index is 6.615, one of the highest in the country. The students pile on AP courses like extra blankets in winter. They almost all get very high scores on the AP tests, so the hard work does not give them much of an advantage in the college competition, but most of them know that learning is more important than polishing their resumes and getting into MIT. "I do not believe that attending a top university will guarantee me a high-paying job or a position of power," said senior Jeffrey S. Cohen. "I believe that the bigger advantage I gain from attending TJ is an intelligent peer group. I think that I can find such a peer group at many universities, and any university where I can find such a group will most likely give me an excellent college experience."

Not all of the nearly three million college freshmen next year will seek the excitement of learning, at least not right away. But most will eventually develop an interest in the intellectual riches they were

A TALE OF TWO DAUGHTERS

Our daughters both graduated from Woodson High School in Fairfax County, Virginia. The older one, who intended to study science and math, got into Cornell but chose McGill. She fell in love with the city of Montreal, with the idea of a school in a very multicultural city where she could walk to the opera and see plays in both French and English. There she studied mathematics and is now head of biostatistics for a French drug company. Her ability to speak French has been as important as her mathematical ability in her work.

My second daughter, first in her class at Woodson, chose the University of Toronto over Yale. There she studied French, classics, and biology. She later attended medical school at McGill and is now in her third year of residency in medicine at the Royal Victoria Hospital.

Finally, we were able to pay all expenses for our daughters' educations while leaving something for retirement. Neither of my daughters would exchange their experiences for four (expensive) years at the Ivy League schools.

—Glenna Hendricks

promised in the college brochure. What is remarkable about American higher education is that most of their colleges will be ready and eager to give them exactly that.

The seniors at Jefferson, Blair, Banneker, and other star schools may have a head start in that search. But their friends in less selective high schools will catch up with them. Fraternity and sorority parties grow stale. Young minds crave nourishment. No matter where they went to high school, they will hear something in a lecture hall that interests them and will spend the rest of their lives exploring and explaining it, turning it into something new.

THE SAT AND
OTHER HIGH
SCHOOL STRESSES

*T*HE SAT WAS in two weeks, softball season had started, the teachers were crazy, and the homework was too much. My daughter's stress meter, she told me, was off the scale. So why was I smiling?

Few times of the year equal the spring months for tension in the households of college-bound teenagers. Books and magazines are full of denunciations of this state of affairs. We are pushing our kids too hard, we are told. Grades matter too much. Standardized testing is out of control. The university admissions process is torture. In one of the latest examples of this mind-set, Denise Clark Pope's wonderfully reported "'Doing School': How We Are Creating a Generation of Stressed Out, Materialistic, and Miseducated Students," the author follows five frantic suburban teenagers and concludes that "we need a new vision of what it means to be successful in school and what it means to be successful in America" (Yale 2001).

THE SAT AS A NECESSARY EVIL

ONE OF THE biggest stresses for college-bound high school students is the SAT test. Now, I don't like the SAT. My distaste for it began when I took it my senior year of high school. As time ran short with too many questions left unanswered, I felt a wave of fear much worse than anything I later experienced as a soldier in Vietnam.

I was like millions of other American teenagers subjected to the SAT and the other college entrance examination, the ACT. I was terrified that a low score would hurt my scholarship chances, make college admission more difficult, and, if the results were really bad, kill my self-confidence and ruin my life.

A generation later, the anxieties have only gotten worse. My daughter and her friends were full of fearful questions about the test before they took it. SAT and ACT preparation courses, such as those run by the *Princeton Review* or my *Washington Post* employers' subsidiary, Kaplan Inc., are thriving. Public schools are forced to schedule courses with titles like "SAT English" to keep the hysteria under control.

Each year about four million teenagers take the ACT or the SAT. The SAT, strongest on the two coasts, used to stand for the Scholastic Aptitude Test and then the Scholastic Assessment Test, but the College Board, tired of the changes and confusion, decided to let the three capital letters stand on their own. ACT, strongest in the middle of the country, once stood for the American College Test but now calls itself simply the ACT Assessment, or ACT for short.

WHAT ARE THE SAT AND ACT ALL ABOUT?

THE SAT-I, called the Reasoning Test by the College Board, is a three-hour mostly multiple-choice test of verbal and mathematical achievement. A revised version, taking effect in March 2005, will add grammar questions, a written essay, and some second-year algebra questions. The ACT is also a three-hour multiple choice test of verbal and mathematical achievement, but it includes science reasoning questions. Overall scores on the SAT can range from 400 to 1,600, with prospective college students hoping for at least 1,000, although many with lower scores are still admitted to some schools. Composite scores on the ACT range from 1 to 36, with a 22 equivalent to a 1,030 on the SAT and a 32 equivalent to a 1,420 on the SAT, the level at which a student has a good chance for admission to the most selective colleges.

It does not matter which test college applicants take, and most go with whichever test is popular at their schools. Some educators think the SAT is more impressive to Ivy League schools, and some think the ACT better measures what is taught in high school courses, but there is little evidence that the choice makes much of a difference. Neither test, college admissions experts say, should be taken more than three times. Two tries is about right, if the student is unhappy with the first score. Plenty of good students are satisfied with the first test result and try no more.

> Some educators think the SAT is more impressive to Ivy League schools, and some think the ACT better measures what is taught in high school courses.

Both the SAT and the ACT are important and can be scary. Although most students handle the pressure with grace and good humor, the sight of an SAT or ACT results envelope generates the same dread as a college acceptance or rejection letter, or the draft board letters that my generation remembers.

I don't mind adolescents getting a good scare. In an academic setting, that often means they have put themselves in a situation where they risk failure, which is usually good for them. What irritates me is young people obsessing over what are, to my mind, mediocre tests.

WHAT'S WRONG WITH THE SAT?

ASIDE FROM A few algebra and geometry questions, the SAT is more or less a long arithmetic, reading, and vocabulary quiz suitable for eighth graders. It has little to do with what high school juniors and seniors are studying. Adding a writing section and some tougher math questions will not improve it very much. (The ACT attempts to test high school subjects in a limited way, so I will leave it be for now, but it shares many of the SAT's problems.)

The SAT was not designed to be a sorting device for all applicants. It was supposed to predict first-year college grades, but it turned out high school grades did that job just as well. Its creators wanted to use it to find a few emeralds in corn silos—students bright enough for the Ivy League but stuck in Midwest high schools Harvard never heard of. Nonetheless, other colleges, always quick to ape the Ivies, adopted the SAT, too.

> Newspapers continue to use SAT results as a measure of school quality, even when a school suffers a decline in its average score only because it has succeeded in persuading lower-achieving students to think about college.

I am galled that newspapers continue to use SAT results as a measure of school quality, even when a school suffers a decline in its average score only because it has succeeded in persuading lower-achieving students to think about college and give the test a try. I am unhappy that many high school juniors add to the already considerable burdens of that most important academic year by enrolling in four-hour-a-week SAT prep courses. I dislike the deeply engrained habit of judging the worth of a college by the average SAT scores of its students.

I think the SAT, or more formally the SAT-I (pronounced "S-A-T-one"), can be supplanted by what were once called the achievement tests and are now called the SAT-IIs. Each SAT-II (pronounced "S-A-T-two" and referred to by the College Board as "Subject Tests") covers a single high school subject, such as American history or writing or biology. Many colleges already require that applicants take at least three of them.

The SAT-IIs make sense to me. They reinforce high school learning.

The student has a choice of subjects. The mystery is, having taken three high school–level examinations like the SAT-IIs, why anyone would need to take an overinflated junior high test like the SAT-I. According to FairTest, a nonprofit organization in Cambridge, Massachusetts, dedicated to reducing the American reliance on testing, nearly three hundred colleges and universities (the College Board says this number is inflated) have made the SAT and the ACT optional for applicants.

But as my daughter Katie got closer to taking the test, I was forced to consider it from an entirely new angle. I realized it was not quite the loathsome canker sore that I had made it out to be. I would still be happy to see both the SAT and the ACT scrapped in favor of high school grades and the results of college-level tests, such as Advanced Placement (AP) and International Baccalaureate (IB), but a note from Kyle Miller, an attorney who teaches SAT preparation classes for Fairfax County, Virginia, made me wonder whether I was seeing the whole picture.

Miller wrote:

If you think parents and kids are stressed out about grades now, wait and see what happens if you make a student's GPA the sole criteria for their college admission. Every grade by every student becomes a potential albatross to a student's chances to get into the college of their dreams. You want principals and teachers dealing with that? What about the anxiety that would cause? At least the SAT offers an opportunity for those students who always seemed to get an 89 instead of a 90 to put up a decent score and get recognized by the Admissions Offices around the country as someone who they would like to include in their freshman class.

He is right. I was proud that my daughter had taken some very difficult courses at a very competitive high school. But that meant she was not likely always to get a top grade. For her and many of her friends, the SAT is an insurance policy that encourages deeper learning and promotes mental health.

If you cannot afford a prep course or agree with me that it is unnecessary, there are plenty of guide books and sample tests at your high school's career center or library. I don't think my daughter needed to take the SAT prep course for which I wrote a large check. But I lacked the intestinal fortitude to tell a twenty-first-century American teenager that she couldn't join her friends in the hunt for higher SAT scores. I muttered about it, but very quietly.

The only bright spot in the gloom of the SAT and ACT obsession is that it certainly doesn't hurt students to add to their vocabulary and brush up their math skills in anticipation of the test, even if there are probably better uses of their time.

I still think we ought to kill SAT stories or bury them deep in the paper. And I think APs, IBs, or SAT-IIs should be substituted for the SAT-I. But until someone figures out a better way to allot limited space in those colleges that have more applicants than seats, I will grudgingly admit that the SAT and the ACT have their uses and wish good luck to Katie and all who follow her, with as much good grace as I can muster.

THE TRUTH ABOUT
HIGH SCHOOL STRESS

SO HOW TRUE are the stories about overwhelmed, overburdened high school students? I have hung out with scores of teenagers as a reporter in the last twenty years, and I don't quite see it that way.

There is SAT or ACT test anxiety, to be sure. But it is fleeting. Few adolescents report that they suffer from lasting academic stress, once they stop trying to convince you that their lives are hell. The Higher Education Research Institute at the University of California at Los Angeles reports that only 34.9 percent of incoming college freshmen in 2001 said they did six or more hours of high school homework a week, the lowest figure since 1987. A survey by New York–based Public Agenda found that 75 percent of high school students felt they would learn more if pushed harder by better teachers.

> Seventy-five percent of high school students felt they would learn more if pushed harder by better teachers.

Critics such as Denise Clark Pope dislike extrinsic rewards—grades and test scores—and prefer that each individual learn, and later work, for the intrinsic value of understanding the world and making it a better place. That is fine, but it fails to address how to divvy up resources. The American formula is pretty simple: If you work hard, you get paid, with extra dollars for unusual creativity and productivity. As a species, we have tried other criteria—noble blood, ethnicity, class background, access to firearms—but none has worked very well.

My daughter and her friends complain that their lives are nothing but a relentless scavenger hunt. But if you listen carefully when they discuss this topic among themselves, there is a different flavor to the conversation. Many of them love the competition. It is not just sixteen-year-old Olympic ice skaters who want to see how good they can be when a medal is on the line. Some courses capture their interest. And they like sharing the fears and strains of getting ready for college and the workplace. They remind me of my nights at Fort Lewis, Washington, in 1967, joining the other draftees in bitching about drill sergeants, mess hall food, and twenty-mile hikes. The stress bonded us as we prepared for the difficult work ahead.

Which is the point, after all. Our children are moving into an adult world where stress is high because we have created so many opportunities for them. They can go anywhere their desires and energies take them. If we want to ease the demands on their time, we should send them to one of the few remaining command economies—Pyongyang is lovely this time of year—where they will have jobs with social and sometimes political sanctions imposed on those who try too hard.

Like Pope, I distrust the way we assess high school students. As I said, the SAT is not a good test. Some class projects are lame. I wish young applicants realized that colleges want to see no more than three or four well-chosen extracurricular activities, rather than a lot of resume padding.

> Colleges want to see no more than three or four well-chosen extracurricular activities, rather than a lot of resume padding.

But once we get the community research projects and internships and other authentic forms of learning that Pope wisely recommends, our children will be just as frazzled and overscheduled as they are now. And that is because *we*—including Pope, who likely found her book a drain on her social life—are frazzled and overscheduled. Those are the lives we want. We have chosen an economic and social system that, though hectic, has proven itself more congenial than any of the likely alternatives.

HOW PARENTS HELP—OR HINDER—THEIR CHILDREN

THERE ARE, OF course, some young people with serious emotional problems who need limits, as well as professional help. But much of the despair I see comes from nothing more than well-meaning parents getting in the way. One of my daughter's friends said her most stressful recent week was the one in which her father insisted she get eight hours of sleep a night. She lost the right to make her own decisions, and the world began to close in. An even more serious problem is parents who tell children who love drama or literature or history that they are going to be doctors or else.

As parents, we tend to forget what it was like to be this young and have to work out a way to handle all the choices of the adult world. We are very susceptible to what I call the "2 A.M. moment," when we get up to go to the bathroom and notice the light is still on under our teenager's door. Uh-oh, we say. She is working too hard. We will have to talk to her about that course. Maybe it is just too much for her.

> As parents, we tend to forget what it was like to be this young and have to work out a way to handle all the choices of the adult world.

What we fail to consider is our feelings about the course that kept *us* up until 2 A.M. when we were that age. More often than not, that is the high school course we remember most fondly, the one with the teacher who demanded the most from us and allowed us to see how much we were capable of. Trying to persuade a student to drop such a course would be a bad idea, to put it mildly.

So I let my daughter do what she wants, including taking an SAT prep course and complaining to me about her life. She seems to be surviving high school, despite all the burdens on her. And she will likely show me exactly how healthy she is, in both body and spirit, when she comes after me for writing this.

4

THE ROLE OF YOUR HIGH SCHOOL COUNSELOR

THE SIDWELL FRIENDS School, a collection of two-story buildings on the upper reaches of Wisconsin Avenue in Washington, D.C., is accustomed to college admissions success. It sent Chelsea Clinton, class of '97, to her first-choice school, Stanford, and did the same for Al Gore III, class of '01, who went to Harvard.

But those two talented graduates had advantages that other Sidwell students, including my daughter Katie, class of '03, do not enjoy. If they want to go to unusually selective colleges like Stanford and Harvard, they have a problem because at Sidwell and other very competitive private and public high schools, there are far more applicants for space in such colleges than the colleges are willing to accept from one school. That means, as proven by the Attewell study described in chapter 2, they are less likely to get into their first-choice college than a similar student at an ordinary public school.

So parents like me get even more anxious, if that is possible. The only offsetting advantage is that schools like Sidwell usually have very good teachers and very good college counselors.

WELCOME TO "PARENTS' NIGHT"

AT AN EVENING meeting in October for junior class parents, the school's two counselors demonstrated what good college guidance entails. I am going to tell you some of what they said, just so you have a benchmark with which to measure the advice you are hearing from the counselors at your high school. Director of college counseling Josh Wolman, a former Columbia University admissions officer, and college counselor Diane Scattergood, an English teacher with a knack for teaching students how to compose their SAT II writing test and application essays, faced about two hundred parents. They had four important messages:

1. **Don't obsess about test scores.** The members of the junior class had just taken the PSAT. The results would come back soon, but Wolman begged the parents not to make a crisis out of the scores, no matter how far they were away from the top score of 240. "You should remember that the PSATs never appear on your child's transcript," he said. "It really is a practice."

To give the parents something to do, a distraction from worrying about the last test, Scattergood told them they could help out by signing their children up for the next test, the SAT in the spring. That would help the juniors stay focused on their studies.

"We don't really want to go to the juniors to tell them, 'You're going to need to sign up for your SATs,'" she said. It was an annoying chore. "But you guys can do that. That would be a nice thing to do."

2. **Don't rush into college discussions and visits.** Wolman reminded the parents that he had once worked in an Ivy League ad-

missions office and knew what those officials would think about high school juniors who showed up while the admissions officers were immersed in the difficult job of figuring out what to do with thousands of high school seniors. "They don't want to see eleventh graders right now," Wolman said. "We are going to have another meeting, one that we look forward to in January, in which we will talk about college visits. I sense the kids don't have any sense of urgency about college right now."

The message was this: It is your children's junior year, their last chance to demonstrate they can achieve in their classes at a level that shows academic talent and determination. The first-term final exams were in January. That was what students should be worrying about.

3. Test prep courses are fine, but they are not essential. Wolman described the courses at the school and the success its teachers had had preparing students for the SAT-I and SAT-II exams. Like most educators, he was not happy about the millions of dollars being spent by American parents on private preparation courses that were not any better, or at least not much better, than the school classes the students were already taking. "You have to trust Sidwell a little bit," Wolman said. "I am not against prep classes. I hope I have made that clear. But you must trust Sidwell a little bit."

Scattergood noted that all the test prep companies were looking for ways to sell their SAT courses. "As you have noticed, they are introducing more every day," she said, lowering her voice to a stage whisper, "because they want money." If a parent and student felt a tutor for an SAT was necessary, Scattergood said, the school had a list of people they trusted.

4. Tests do count, but so do grades and extracurricular activities. A parent saw an inconsistency in what Sidwell's high school principal had said at a previous meeting about the concern over high-stakes testing. "At the last meeting we were discouraged from doing any prep work for the SAT, and now you are encouraging it," she said.

Wolman sighed. "The reality is, the tests count," he said. "We are faced with that right now with the seniors. We have schools making tough choices, in part based on those tests. There is a fine line. The tests count, but they shouldn't run their lives."

Extracurricular activities were particularly important, he said, and a few intense activities are better than many shallow enterprises. "The key word is *passion*," Wolman said. "And you can't be passionate about ten things when you are sixteen years old. And it has to be demonstrated passion. We want that."

The evening was winding down. The parents seemed resigned to a year and a half of anxiety and miscommunication with their children. Scattergood, sensing the mood, tried to cheer them up. "Don't worry," she said. "You don't get such opportunities often to share things with your kids. It is a time to go places and talk about important things. This should be fun."

IS YOUR HIGH SCHOOL COUNSELOR GOOD ENOUGH?

MY HIGH SCHOOL guidance counselor, Mr. Stretch, was as demanding as his name suggested. But he had dealt with enough hormone-addled teenagers to know he had to cloak his strong views in whimsy and understatement.

I remember storming into his office to complain about a Latin teacher who had failed to give me the A my obvious brilliance deserved. He was sympathetic but also amused. The teacher, he knew, delighted in giving first-semester Bs to grade freaks like me. The teacher called us "millimeter bandits." Mr. Straight told me not to worry and, deftly changing the subject, asked how my algebra class—where I was the acknowledged teacher's pet—was going.

When it came time to apply to colleges, he was similarly calm and reassuring. He knew I was frightened by the megacampuses like Berkeley that my friends were applying to. He steered me toward

KEEPING YOUR PERSPECTIVE: POINTERS FOR PARENTS

✦   Don't obsess about test scores.

✦   Don't rush into college discussions and visits.

✦   Test prep courses are fine but they aren't essential.

✦   Tests do count, but so do grades and extracurricular activities.

warm little schools, Pomona and Occidental, which would give me time to figure out who I was and what I wanted to do.

Approximately one hundred thousand high school counselors now offer the same soothing advice to a new generation of high school students. Each spring their patience is severely tested by students who want someone to blame when they don't get into the colleges they have lusted after since eighth grade.

Counselors do make mistakes. I watched the hilarious film *Orange County,* in which Lily Tomlin plays a counselor who mistakenly switches the transcripts of the school's leading scholar and its least ambitious slacker. I remembered the much sadder case of a counselor at Mamaroneck High School, a New York suburban high school where I once spent a lot of time. She had had a splendid career, helping many adolescents cut through all the hyperbole about certain schools. But one year—shortly after her husband died—she wrote up recommendations for the school's best journalist using information from the file of another girl with a similar name. She became the butt of wicked jokes throughout the parent grapevine, even though the affected student still got into Cornell.

Counselors vary in quality. Some do not deal well with certain kinds of students. Some have bad years. Some are distracted by family problems. But they are usually good-hearted people who like students. They are quick to respond to family emergencies and emotional crises. They also will cover for other counselors who are having their own problems, without making too much of a fuss about it.

These days one of the most important requirements for a good counselor, as well as a good teacher, is stamina. There is no substitute for a classroom teacher who is willing to put in the added hours that make learning work for struggling kids. That is particularly true for high school counselors, who in most cases are responsible for more than three hundred students each year.

> One of the most important requirements for a good counselor, as well as a good teacher, is stamina.

It is not just a matter of scheduling office hours into the night. The students who need help the most are often the ones least likely to show up. The effective counselor is willing to get out of her office and check out the football bleachers, the back of the gym, and the clump of smokers out on the curb to find her counselee.

The other requirements for counselors are what they have always been—sense of humor, love of kids, intimate knowledge of the strengths and weaknesses of the faculty, and a good sense of each student's family background and academic history. And then, when it comes to colleges, each counselor has to understand the admissions process and how best to communicate with the college admissions officers who are going to be making the decisions.

COUNSELORS AND THE COLLEGE ADMISSIONS PROCESS

A FEW SCHOOLS in communities where college admission is the number one priority have put their counselors on a very high pedestal. Scarsdale High School in Westchester County, New York, for instance, does not use the title "counselor." The educators responsible for advising students on their academic lives and university choices are called "deans," and each one has a caseload of no more than two hundred students.

For the most motivated and mature students, counselors become almost superfluous. High school college and career centers—as well as Websites, libraries, and bookstores—are overflowing with guides to colleges. The Internet has made university Web pages, many of them bottomless pits of information, quickly accessible to most people.

For a student with his or her goals firmly in mind, one twenty-minute conversation with a counselor is probably enough. The counselor can share her views on which colleges seem to match the student's interests and assess the student's chances of admission at each school based on how previous applicants with similar records at that school have done. The rest is just filling in the forms and praying to the admissions gods for favorable decisions.

For the many students who are not so eager to take charge of their academic future, a longer session with the counselor is a must. Smart high schools schedule an initial meeting between counselor and student, and then a follow-up meeting with the student's parents. This lets the counselor sense the student's feelings unfiltered by parental ambitions and allows for much better advice.

Parents should make sure their children take the PSAT in the fall of their junior year, and each junior with an interest in college should have a conversation on the subject with their counselor no later than January of the junior year. That will allow the counselor to make certain they are signed up for the SAT or ACT that spring and to begin discussing their collegiate desires. Admissions experts say parents should meet with their child's counselor sometime in the junior year, and no later than October of the senior year, after student and counselor have had that first meeting. It is a family activity, and although the student will have the final say (limited by the available financial resources), the parents need to understand the process and how they fit in before early acceptance deadlines in November.

That leads to what is the crucial question about college counseling in the twenty-first century: Should you hire a private college admissions counselor? You can find them in the Yellow Pages under "Educational Consultants." Most have a basic one-meeting consultation charge, which can be as low as $300. And a few charge as much as $400 an hour, the rate of the popular Manhattan consultant whom *New York* magazine revealed charged some affluent parents as much as $28,000 for weekly services stretching over more than a year.

It's your money. If it makes you more comfortable to spend it on a private counselor who is probably no more competent than your school counselor, go right ahead. I am the guy who handed his daugh-

WHAT HAPPENS WHEN? A TIMETABLE FOR WORKING WITH YOUR HIGH SCHOOL COUNSELOR

✦ A student should sign up to take the PSAT in the fall of his junior year.

✦ The student should talk with his counselor about college choices and goals no later than January of his junior year. This conversation may work best without parents present so the counselor can accurately assess the student's own needs and hopes.

✦ Sign up for the SAT and/or ACT in the spring of junior year.

✦ Parents should arrange to meet with the counselor about college options during their child's junior year or no later than October of their senior year.

✦ Carefully weigh the benefits before hiring a private college admissions counselor.

ter $975 for an SAT prep course that I did not think she needed, so I am not qualified to preach frugality and limits in an age of excess. And I am moved by the desire of some parents to have a designated professional do the nagging as application deadlines approach so that family harmony, what there is of it at this age, is preserved.

Perhaps a counselor's most important function is to be another voice, a third party to listen to both parents and student and make sure everyone stays on track. College discussion should not focus on the hideous state of the college applicant's room or the fashion choices of his girlfriend or the amount of time he is spending at the mall. The idea is to determine which of his or her interests are most important in making a college selection, and then compiling a list of likely places to research and, when possible, visit. It is also, of course, a discussion of deadlines and essay writing, and choices of teachers to make recommendations, which can be troublesome and sometimes requires someone other than the parent to be the monitoring agent.

Some public high school counselors are willing and able to play that role. If parents think their child needs that kind of help and do not feel comfortable doing it themselves, they should ask the counselor if she would be willing to put their child on her list of cases that need special handling. If she says yes, and a check with other parents reveals that her word is good, then the problem is solved. If not, an older sibling or other relative or family friend may sometimes fill the role. And if that is not an option, get out your checkbook.

Parents of teenagers know they are often disqualified from receiving important information and dispensing vital advice to their children because they are just too insufferable. When I was at Mamaroneck High working on a book about high schools, I had a child of my own in another high school who told me next to nothing about what was going on. It was refreshing, after the silent treatment at home, to wander the halls of Mamaroneck and listen to students share their deepest fears and ambitions. When I interviewed their parents, they would beg for tidbits from my discussions with their children, expressing their relief when I informed them that their child's goals were pretty close to what they wished for.

For the moment, you may have to hire an independent voice, a human bridge over your troubled waters. Once your children begin the journey with their own children, they will realize how horribly they behaved and may even tell you so.

GOOD HIGH SCHOOL COUNSELORS AT WORK

ONE DAY IN the fall of 1995, college counselors at one of Washington's best-known private schools totaled the results of a student survey and found, to their shock, that twenty-seven seniors, more than 20 percent of the class, said they were planning to apply to one very selective two-hundred-year-old New England institution, Bowdoin College.

Such a massive rush at one small undergraduate institution had never happened at the Washington school before. The counseling staff wondered what to do. Bowdoin, they were certain, would never accept even half that many students from one place. "Bowdoin was too small a school to risk having its freshman class dominated by one high school," a counselor said.

The school staff tried to suggest, very gently, that some of the applicants look around for good alternatives. This is something counselors are doing with increasing frequency, particularly at the magnet and private high schools that harbor so many students with Ivy ambitions. Yet the students and their parents remain so focused on the most oversubscribed schools that the gridlock is getting worse.

The Paul Attewell study I discussed in chapter 2 says that despite the many advantages of attending the most challenging and competitive high schools, students with similar test scores at more modest secondary schools have a better chance of getting into the most sought-after colleges. Because more students at the most competitive high schools apply to selective colleges in greater numbers than do students at neighborhood high schools, and since selective colleges are reluctant to take more than a handful of students from any one school, there is a problem for students at high schools like the one with twenty-seven seniors wanting to go to Bowdoin.

How do counselors at very competitive high schools handle the overload of applicants to Dartmouth, Stanford, or the University of Chicago? And how can a student who finds himself in this traffic jam maintain his sanity and his friendships, and still get into a good college?

Katherine Cohen, the founder of the New York–based counseling practice, IvyWise, encountered the problem when she was in high school. Cohen attended the Westlake School, a very competitive private school in Los Angeles. She had a grade point average of 3.99 plus many Advanced Placement courses, an American Field Service summer in Argentina, a photography portfolio, and extensive dance experience. But her counselor said she ranked only eighth in a class of ninety. Her hopes of attending Brown, the counselor said, were unrealistic because there were two other applicants in her class with what the counselor thought were better records.

KEEPING THE BALANCE: WHAT COUNSELORS CAN DO TO HELP STUDENTS

WAS THE COUNSELOR wise to be so discouraging? Private school and magnet school counselors say they owe such students and their families their best assessments of their chances, when asked, but acknowledge the conversations can get tense. "Parents and students are told of the likelihood of Johnny being accepted," said one college counselor at a Washington area magnet school, "but some really think they are entitled to admission in any case."

This only aggravates adolescent competitive instincts and insecurities. Sally O'Rourke, a counselor at Andover High School in

Massachusetts, a public school, said, "I had one student ask me to swear that I wouldn't tell anyone where she was applying early before she would tell me. She was paranoid about it." A counselor at a Maryland private school said one of her students concluded that a good friend had stolen the idea of applying to a certain selective college. "She felt very violated," the counselor said, "because she had a longtime interest in this college, and she felt that her friend's interest was not thought out, that the other girl was avoiding doing any personal soul-searching and only applying because it was the easiest and most appealing course of action."

To that counselor's relief, both students got into the selective school, but often the competition does not end so happily.

If you or your child doesn't attend a competitive high school, or if you believe as I do that many lesser-known colleges are just as good as the brand names, then no worries. But that kind of attitude is not so common among the parents and students at the most intensely academic high schools.

At Andover High, O'Rourke said, the staff has done two things she thinks help. First, like many competitive high schools, they eliminated class rankings so colleges cannot place too much weight on how each student's grades compare. Second, they show students and their families a book they have compiled of the grades and scores of the students accepted from that school by each college, without revealing the students' names. "Then they make their own decisions," she said. A counselor at a Washington, D.C., private school said the furthest she will go is "if no one is applying to a school that would normally have applicants from us, we tell the class that they seem to be overlooking the place."

Letitia W. Peterson, the director of college counseling at the Holton-Arms School in Bethesda, Maryland, said, "In a climate where counselors are already feeling pressure caused by the frenzy surrounding admissions, the perception that we somehow prioritize the applicants may create more anxiety, animosity, and eventually, blame. It is normal for most seventeen-year-olds to have mixed emotions about their decision making, and they need to have their counselor as an ally and confidant, not view us as partner to an impersonal and judgmental process."

WHAT STUDENTS CAN DO

SO IF YOU are a student, trapped in a crush of classmates trying to wedge themselves into your favorite school, what should you do?

You can either prepare to accept your fate, knowing that these decisions are unpredictable and that your second-choice college is a fine institution, or you can do everything you can to demonstrate that you want your first-choice school more than your competitors do.

Cohen got into Brown early action (we'll explore the early action and early decision processes later in the book) by visiting the school twice, getting to know the admissions officers there, crafting the best possible essay, and leaving no doubt of her passion for that university. She still has unpleasant memories of the counselor who suggested she was an also-ran, but she warns clients in a similar jam that the worst thing they could do would be to thumb their noses at their high school counselors.

> You should do everything you can to demonstrate that you want your first-choice school more than your competitors do.

Instead, she says, they should try to change their counselors' minds, while they continue to make their cases directly to the colleges. Having gone through Cohen's exhaustive process of imagining they are already attending the colleges of their choice, her clients go to their college counselors with eye-popping presentations of what they want and how that particular school fulfills their needs. "This process has swayed many a counselor," Cohen said. When the college admissions officer asks that counselor about that student, he is likely to be much higher on her list.

Still, even with the most passionate presentations, most of those twenty-seven students who wanted to go to Bowdoin College were not likely to live their dream. Their high school's counselors opted to state the facts and let them draw their own conclusions. "We went to a senior class meeting and told them that, even if every one of their applications were stunning, Bowdoin would never be able to accept the majority of them," one counselor said.

Only three students dropped out of the race at that point. Bowdoin noted the quality of the high school and the great interest of the applicants, and it took an unusually large number, seven. But that was as far as the college could go. And, the counselor recalled, "We have never had that kind of interest in Bowdoin again. Where did that come from? What goes on in the minds of teenagers?"

She said she didn't know but was preparing for more gridlock. "The whole system has been caught in an inflationary spiral," she said. "The colleges say they have more applications than ever, so it's more competitive to get in, so kids feel they need to apply to more schools. If that cycle remains unchecked, I don't see how anyone will be able to manage this process."

But there are ways for each family to take control of their own admissions process to avoid the most destructive pressures and make the best choice.

HEATHER'S ADVENTURE, PART 2

Heather thought Davidson was too small. It was no bigger than her high school, which had 1,600 students. She shed her passive approach to college searching and announced that less was not more. The small schools were out, despite her parents' feeling that she needed a cozy environment.

On visits to relatives in the Midwest, she saw Washington University of St. Louis and Northwestern. She rejected Northwestern, but thought she might apply to WUSL in hopes of winning a scholarship. She looked at Cornell, which seemed too cold. She thought the University of Virginia was okay, but then it was essentially an annex of her celebrated high school, Jefferson in Fairfax County. Every year, about a hundred Jefferson students, a quarter of the graduating class, went to Mr. Jefferson's university, happy to pay in-state tuition to such a fine school.

She decided the New England states were too chilly. She would go no farther north than Princeton, which she liked, and the University of Pennsylvania, which she loved. It was that affection for Penn that caused all the trouble.

Her parents hated Penn. Her mother thought the campus, in a somewhat seedy if colorful Philadelphia neighborhood, was dangerous, and disliked its setup, with a beautiful, open academic quad surrounded by dormitories in "lockdown." Her father thought the university, particularly its Wharton business school where Heather planned to take courses, was a moral sinkhole. He had met some unethical business people who had gone to Wharton, and he blamed their school for that disdain for the Golden Rule.

Her mother feared for her body and mind. Her father feared for her soul. They forbade her decision to apply to Penn early, as Heather would have preferred to do. So she did not apply anywhere early, trusting in her counselor's view that she was such a good candidate it would not matter when she applied. She had 1,520 SAT scores. Her grade point average was 4.04 at one of the most academically demanding schools in the country. She had her singing and cheerleading and riding and other leadership activities. No one could foresee that that would not be enough.

5

THE SEARCH
LETTER SCAM

*T*HE LETTER MICHAEL Eisenbrey received his junior year in high school, at least as his mother remembers it, seemed to guarantee admission to Carleton College, one of the most sought-after schools in the country. "It said you are the type of student we want at Carleton," said his mother, Barbara Somson. Other letters followed, as well as invitations to Carleton get-togethers in the Washington area. "They were recruiting me," Michael said.

That was no surprise. His PSAT scores were high enough to make him a National Merit semifinalist. His SAT score, the first and only time he took it in the spring of his junior year, was 1,590. He was active in drama productions and had a splendid grade point average.

So why did Michael, fifteen months later, receive from Carleton's Northfield, Minnesota, campus not the warm offer of admission he expected but a sadly polite letter saying he had been put on the waiting list? After sending him the equivalent of candy and flowers, after declaring its devotion and dropping hints of a long-term relation-ship, why did Carleton decide it didn't have room for him? Why such a big tease from an otherwise reputable and admirable school?

I have long been curious about these gushy missives—the col-leges call them "search letters"—that arrive in the mailboxes of high school juniors and seniors with impressive PSAT and SAT scores. The marketing executives for some of our nation's finest institutions of higher learning seem to be making promises that their admissions officers can't keep.

> The marketing execu-tives for some of our nation's finest institu-tions of higher learning seem to be making promises that their admissions officers can't keep.

Michael, who was then a senior at George-town Day School in Washington, couldn't find his copies of the original correspondence from Carleton, but I have been compiling my own collection of college love notes received by high-scoring high schoolers. Here are some excerpts. Read them and decide for yourself if they sound like pick-up lines at very reputable taverns:

Listen: College admission people all over the country, including me, have decided that you are the kind of smart student they want.
—Paul Marthers, dean of admission,
Reed College, Portland, Oregon

Bright, high-achieving students like you have lots of college op-tions to choose from. If you'll stop for a moment and peel back the front cover of Hopkins, you'll find there are many intriguing ways to: [followed by a list of the school's many programs and courses].
—John Latting, director of undergraduate
admissions, Johns Hopkins University

I'm looking for the next set of stars, the students who are the best of their generation, who are prepared to actively shape this nation—and this planet—in this new millennium. Students with the potential and desire to become the best at whatever they do. Your PSAT scores indicate that you may be among these special people. If so, I believe that MIT may be the place for you—where you can fully explore all of your potential and develop your talents.

—Marilee Jones, dean of admissions,
Massachusetts Institute of Technology

Each year Wellesley College receives a list of especially accomplished and able young women from the Student Search Service of the College Board. These are the kinds of women we hope will apply to Wellesley, and your name is on this year's list.

—Janet Lavin Rapelye, dean of admission,
Wellesley College

We congratulate you on your impressive academic record and encourage you to consider Yale.

—Richard H. Shaw, dean of admissions
and financial aid, Yale University

By the way, Shaw enclosed a decal of Handsome Dan, the Yale bulldog mascot, with the words "Congratulations from Yale" printed on it. It was suitable for putting on your car window, presumably so all your friends would know that the application process, at least for you, was a mere formality.

I have more examples, and my collection is far from complete. Some are more egregious than others. Students and their families have varying reactions to these florid valentines. Some write them off as advertising, like time-share companies promising trips to Florida. Others give them more credence.

Andrew Furlow, a high-scoring junior in Arlington, Virginia, received search letters from Amherst, Tufts, Chicago, and other prestigious colleges. But the one that caught his eye came from Brown University—"one of those schools that 'almost no one' got into," he said. No one promised him anything, but receiving the letter raised his hopes. So it was upsetting when Brown deferred him after he applied for early decision and then rejected him in the spring.

Amadie Hart, a Falls Church, Virginia, resident, recalled being induced to apply to the Massachusetts Institute of Technology by a search letter—and then rejected. Although she did well at the University of California at Santa Barbara, she said she was annoyed that MIT officials "said they wanted me and then decided that they didn't, especially after a particularly grueling application process."

John Van Eck, now working for the Montgomery County, Maryland, government, remembers nearly drowning in the deluge of search letters sparked by his high PSAT scores when he was a very bright student attending a high school in Wisconsin that didn't send many students to brand-name colleges. Each said "they were the greatest place on Earth; I was great for them; they wanted me."

Unfortunately, neither he nor his parents had much experience with college recruiting. "At sixteen, I was not prepared to analyze the choices," he said. He made what he later realized was an ill-considered decision to go to a school, the University of Wisconsin at Madison, that was too big for him. Eventually he had to transfer to Susquehanna University to get the kind of education he wanted.

WHAT DO SEARCH LETTERS REALLY MEAN?

THE USE OF search letters has grown enormously in the past several decades. When students take the PSAT their junior year of high school and the SAT after that, they often mark the box that allows the College Board to send their addresses to schools looking for prospective applicants. The ACT Assessment test operates in a similar way. Colleges buy the College Board or ACT lists, often focusing on high scorers, minorities, or students with particular interests. In recent years, some experts say, the marketing executives who help compose the search letters have let their soap-selling instincts get the better of them.

"They have become more aggressive," said Diane Epstein, a Bethesda-based educational consultant who has advised college applicants for nearly a quarter century. She said she tells her young clients, "Look, it's flattering, but take it with a grain of salt."

But the college officials responsible for these come-ons say they don't see anything wrong with them. Sarah Maxwell, Carleton's director of media relations, said, "Our admissions goal is to target students who might be a good fit at Carleton and present the College honestly to them. Any student going through our admissions process is made aware of our selectivity and the factors we consider for each prospective student."

> The marketing executives who help compose the search letters have let their soap-selling instincts get the better of them.

Marthers at Reed said setting the right tone was "tricky," but the schools just want to get good students on their mailing lists so they can be fully informed. "At Reed we want to get the student's attention, say something that makes Reed distinctive and memorable," he said. Dennis O'Shea, a spokesperson for Johns Hopkins, said the letters are designed to encourage good students who might otherwise be intimidated by a famous college name and not apply. He said he agreed that schools should not promise more than they can deliver, but "I don't think our letter does that."

There is evidence that some good students are reluctant to apply to the best-known schools without encouragement. Gretchen Hoff, a 1996 graduate of Bullard High School in Fresno, California, said she would never have applied to Harvard University, where she graduated in 2000, if it had not been for what she called the school's "glowing recruitment letter."

College officials also reject the frequent charge that they just want to make money from the additional application fees and look good in college-rating guides that give points to the schools that reject the most students. Perhaps their motives are as pure as they say, but I wonder whether they have thought carefully about the impression search letters create in the often naive minds of their young targets and their inexperienced parents.

> Selective schools cannot guarantee that students who get a high PSAT score in the fall of their junior year are going to be admitted.

As Michael Eisenbrey's example shows, selective schools cannot guarantee that students who get a high PSAT score in the fall of their junior year are going to be admitted. For the rest of this decade, as a huge clump of American adolescents, the children of the postwar baby boomers, works its way through high school and the college admissions process, there will be more applicants than there have ever been for the most well-known and prestigious schools. Such schools do not admit students based on PSAT, SAT, or ACT scores alone. High scores and grades only get you tossed in the "possible" pile. The final decisions depend heavily on essays, teacher recommendations, and extracurricular activities. And putting someone on the waiting list, as we shall see in chapter 13, is usually just a polite way of saying no.

READING—OR FINDING— THE FINE PRINT

I STILL HOPE, each time I read one of these warm and inviting missives to high test scorers that I will find somewhere in the letter some sort of cautionary word or disclaimer. How hard would it be to say something like this? "Of course, we look at much more than PSAT scores, so please do not take this letter as a promise of admission." Or perhaps this: "We get far more applicants than we have spaces, and admission is not guaranteed, but we hope you will give us a try."

So far I have found only one college, Harvard, that provides such a warning in more than one hundred search letters I have read. Whenever I look at these missives, I feel like I am scanning the latest prize announcement from whatever magazine sales enterprise has added me to their list. The million-dollar check seems to be mine, until I remember reading news stories about the literal-minded people, somewhat elderly like me, who turned up at contest offices and were told that they had misinterpreted the language.

Perhaps not as many people are fooled by these mash notes as one would think. Twenty-first-century American teenagers, particularly those with high PSAT scores, are by and large a realistic bunch. Abigail Ellsworth, now the reference librarian for a Washington law firm, said she devised an aggressive sorting system when the flood of search letters reached her mailbox. "If it didn't have my name on the front, I threw it out," she said. "If the letter itself said 'Dear Student' or 'Dear High School Senior/Junior,' I threw it out. If it addressed me as 'Miss Ellsworth' instead of 'Ms. Ellsworth' or 'Abigail,' I threw it out. If it spoke directly to my overall SAT score and not my particular interests, I threw it out."

But when you add the party invitations and personal letters from leading alumni and special summer school brochures that often follow the initial congratulatory letters, it is difficult for even the most hard-headed high school student to accept the notion that a wait-list or rejection letter is still possible.

Barbara Somson, Michael Eisenbrey's mother, said she "felt sort of jilted" when the wait-list letter arrived from Carleton. Michael was less upset. "I was disappointed," he said, but he had already gotten into his first-choice school, Macalester College of St. Paul, Minnesota.

Mother and son say they think he may have been punished for not attending the local Carleton parties he was invited to. That may have been interpreted as a sign that the school was not his first choice, a key ingredient in the alchemy of the admissions process, as we shall see in chapter 10.

On this issue, the admissions directors and deans beg for understanding. Shaw at Yale said his letter and the decal were designed to celebrate the recipient's good test scores and grades, not promise admission. Some college officials rejected the idea of warning recipients that the letter was not promise of admission. They said even the slightest discouraging word might keep a good candidate from filling out an application. But Shaw, along with Marthers at Reed and Jones at MIT, said they thought it worthwhile at least to consider adding some cautionary language.

> Even the slightest discouraging word might keep a good candidate from filling out an application.

The effect of the letters is still something of a mystery, with little research to guide the debate. Furlow, the Arlington student, was happy to be accepted by Duke after Brown turned him down, but he still wondered at his strong reaction to the Brown search letter. Why had he let his hopes get so high?

He concluded it was not just the Ivy League school's marketing campaign but the cumulative effect of all the search letters. "Brown's letter did not convince me I would be admitted to Brown, but the mass of letters from every possible source altogether made me feel invincible when it came to college admissions," he said.

Spreading good cheer and self-confidence is good, as long as everybody is clear about the chances of getting into the schools that send out search letters. I still think a warning sentence would reduce considerably the sense of ultimate betrayal. The fine colleges who market themselves this way may be teaching students through painful experience the dangers of accepting praise at face value, but I don't think that is what they had in mind.

6

RANKINGS, SAT SCORES, AND FINANCES

What to Consider in Selecting Your College

*T*EST SCORES AND the cost of a college education are obvious factors in narrowing the field of college possibilities, and we will examine them shortly. In many American homes, however, one of the key resources in selecting a college is *U.S. News and World Report's* "America's Best Colleges" list. But just how valuable is it in the complex process of applying for college admission? In 1996, a year before he graduated from Stanford University, Nick Thompson began to think the nation's most popular college-rating guide might not be the best thing for either colleges or the young people they had vowed to educate.

He had not used the "America's Best Colleges" list when he was in high school. He had picked Stanford, his father's alma mater, for its track program, its environmental science courses, and the oak-studded beauty of the surrounding mountains. Besides, he didn't get into his other two top choices.

But in 1996, about the time he was elected Stanford student body vice president, he became aware of how much impact the *U.S. News*–ranked list of colleges was having. He saw a copy of the magazine's annual late-summer college issue on his little sister's bedroom floor. She told him it was the Bible for her and her friends making college decisions. When he earned money for one of the student organizations by manning the Stanford alumni fund-raising phone bank, he was startled to hear the supervisor say, "Tell them that even if they give only one dollar it will help our ranking." Sure enough, he checked and it was true. The portion of alumni giving money to the college was one of the factors measured by *U.S. News,* and Stanford's record was not as good as many of its rivals.

I doubt that your family, any more than mine, will be able to resist the temptation to see how the schools on your list rate in *U.S. News.* As someone who has tried in a very limited way to rate high schools, I don't see anything wrong with making comparisons based on carefully explained data. Readers can decide for themselves whether the rankings have merit.

So I have little quarrel with "America's Best Colleges." Still, the story of Thompson and his battle with *U.S. News* illustrates vividly both the strengths and weaknesses of the list, and why it should not count for as much as it does in some homes.

WHAT DOES THE LIST REALLY MEASURE?

IN THE VIEW of the editors of *U.S. News* and the many families who have used their guide since 1983, there is nothing wrong with summarizing the qualities of a college with statistics. Before the *U.S. News* rankings began, applicants had to rely on rumor, intuition, their own inexact comparisons of the numbers they found in the existing college guides, and their high school counselor's judgment in determining which colleges offered the most.

Not only did the magazine dare to rank schools, but it also forced colleges to begin presenting data on SAT averages, faculty backgrounds, and admissions decisions in a consistent way or be left off the *U.S. News* list altogether. The magazine acknowledged that it could not quantify every factor that made a good school. It had trouble finding measures of the quality of learning and campus life once students enrolled. But it made some progress—forcing colleges to compile and release the percent of their students who graduated in six years, a useful indicator of a university's commitment to ensuring each student's success.

According to *U.S. News,* "When consumers invest in simple household appliances, this sort of information is freely available. We think it should be similarly available for an educational investment that can cost more than $110,000" (1996 edition of "America's Best Colleges").

THOMPSON'S WAR AGAINST "AMERICA'S BEST COLLEGES"

FOR THOMPSON AND a growing number of students and college administrators who would soon respond to his call for action against the list, the *U.S. News* statement was not sensible consumerism but callous disregard of the unique character of American higher education. Thompson became convinced that Stanford, as well as many other universities, was making decisions based less on the welfare of its students and more on its financial health and national reputation. It seemed to him that every major decision was aimed in some way at making Stanford look better in the rankings, and thus getting more people to give money to the already wealthy and rapidly growing campus in the foothills of the San Francisco peninsula.

Historically, Stanford had tried to ignore the *U.S. News* list. In the list's first year, when Stanford was rated number one among undergraduate institutions, Pres. Donald Kennedy, at the urging of

Stanford spokesperson Robert Beyers, called the magazine rankings a "beauty contest." He said it did not have much significance. But by 1996, the university had slipped to number 6, and Thompson thought he saw several indications that officials cared about that ranking and wanted to fix it.

The university grading policy had become stricter. The tenure system seemed designed to lure and keep famous professors, not good teachers. Interesting curricular experiments, such as letting undergraduates major in fields that cut across several disciplines, were in trouble.

Most important to Thompson, the university had rejected a proposal he had made to create what he called "a socially responsible endowment fund." The idea had come from his earlier efforts with many other students to persuade Stanford to sell its stock in companies still doing business with the vicious military government of Myanmar, formerly known as Burma. They wanted alumni to have the option of directing their university contributions to a stock fund cleansed of companies that polluted the environment or supported governments that violated human rights. But university officials said no, and Thompson thought part of the reason was that they did not want to look too radical in the eyes of the deans at other universities who participated in the annual academic reputation ratings that had the heaviest weight in the *U.S. News* rankings. Even more important, he thought, was Stanford's reluctance to do anything that might at all adversely affect the percentage of alumni who donated, its weakest category in the rankings.

Thompson sent an op-ed piece to the *Los Angeles Times* saying what he felt about all this. His attack on the leading guide for what many middle-class families thought was the most important decision of their lives was irresistible to the American media, and the *Times* was

> Thompson became convinced that Stanford, as well as many other universities, was making decisions based less on the welfare of its students and more on its financial health and national reputation.

the first to succumb. The op-ed piece, which ran on October 6, 1996, began, "My 17 year old sister has a collage of teenage vices strewn across her floor: cool Absolut Vodka advertisements, magazines with anorexic women on the cover and, the craftiest demon of them all, *U.S. News & World Report*'s guide to 'America's Best Colleges.'"

He recounted what he considered the ratings' poisonous influence on Stanford. He called this an attempt "to 'Harvardize' what has been a unique and pioneering institution." He called on *U.S. News* to do what other guides do: present the information they have on colleges in alphabetical order, not ranks. "The rankings are arbitrary and absurdly counter-intuitive in their yearly variance," he said.

> Can a stable university like Johns Hopkins really change from
> being the 21st best school in the nation to the 10th and then back
> to 15th in a three year period? However, they are taken as dogma
> by many college applicants. Consequently, many impressionable
> young students, often egged on by their overbearing parents,
> choose colleges based on the rankings of *U.S. News,* not based
> on what is best for themselves and their individual needs.

The article was a sensation. Egged on by e-mails Thompson had sent to other student leaders around the country, dozens of college newspapers editorialized in favor of his initiative. An organization was formed, the Forget *U.S. News* Coalition (FUNC). Student governments passed supportive resolutions. Within weeks the campaign was featured in the Associated Press, the *New York Times,* the *San Francisco Chronicle,* and dozens of other outlets.

Stanford president Gerhard Casper surprised Thompson and the other movement leaders by expressing sympathy for their cause. Casper issued a statement saying that by ranking schools, "*U.S. News* does a substantial disservice to prospective students and fails to meet basic standards of good social science and journalism." He said the university was establishing a new Website to display useful statistics on Stanford that would be free to all and unfiltered by *U.S. News*'s weighting system. He said Stanford would still submit "objective data" to the magazine, but its officials would no longer participate in the *U.S. News* survey asking them to rate the academic reputations of other schools, which he called "subjective reputational votes."

But that was about as far as it went. Interest in the antirankings campaign faded when Thompson and other activists graduated the next year. The popularity of the *U.S. News* list continued to grow, pushing sales up 40 percent for the late-summer edition that announced the new rankings. The list drew eight million visitors to the magazine's Website (www.usnews.com).

A few years after he left Stanford, Thompson took a few more swipes at *U.S. News,* this time from his position as an editor and writer for the *Washington Monthly.* In 2000 he revealed that an internal report commissioned by *U.S. News* had found that the weights given to each factor used in the ratings lacked "any defensible empirical or theoretical basis." In 2001 he upbraided *U.S. News* for not including some of the student surveys that were being collected by a coalition of colleges and universities looking for better ways to describe themselves to applicants.

But it was an older, less angry Thompson who wrote those stories. "I had become convinced the rankings could be a good thing— if only *U.S. News* would do them right," he said. "While at Stanford, I had argued that something like college experience just couldn't be quantified."

I don't think either the rankings or the antiranking views of many educators and activists like Thompson have had much effect on how American families think about colleges. The very selective schools that dominate the list were considered the best schools in the country before the list existed. They will remain so as long as they say no to the vast majority of their applicants. "Your reputation is set by whom you reject, not whom you accept," said C.D. Mote, the president of the University of Maryland–College Park, which has been doing well

lately on the *U.S. News* lists. "The more you reject, the better your reputation."

It is self-fulfilling prophecy. The more students who are excluded from the freshman class,
the higher will be that class's average SAT scores,
yield, and several other factors that influence the
U.S. News ratings.

I think the wisest students and their parents
already know what to do with the list. They
glance at the ratings each year, note the statistics about the schools
that interest them, read the usually well-nuanced articles that ac-
company the lists, and go back to making their own plans.

> The wisest students and their parents already know what to do with the list.

BUT WHAT ABOUT MY SAT SCORES?

A COLLEGE, LIKE a new suit, has to fit. I don't care if it is number
one on the *U.S. News & World Report* list and has an endowment of
$20 billion. If it doesn't offer the courses and activities that feed your
soul, it is no good. If the dorms are awash in alcohol and you only
drink tea, if there is no football team and you ache to yell your lungs
out on Saturday afternoon, if the economics department is Keyne-
sian and Milton Friedman is your man, go somewhere else.

Unfortunately, many seventeen-year-olds don't enjoy analyzing
their likes and dislikes in such detail. I was like that when I was that
age, and the teenagers I know today are the same. They will latch
onto two or three things that strike them as pleasing or annoying but
not conduct a full audit. And they will let other people set their
agendas for them, including the college recruiters and tour guides
who want them to choose a particular school.

Consider one important characteristic of a college—the level of
academic challenge. See how twisted the arguments can become

if a student does not think clearly about his or her personal comfort level.

George Mason University professor and columnist Walter E. Williams, with an economist's distaste for misallocated resources, says high school students should not apply to—and their parents should not pay tuition for—colleges whose average SAT scores are two hundred points or more higher than theirs.

Not a problem, you say. You sent that application to Dartmouth only because you liked the idea of getting a classy Ivy League rejection letter. But don't be so sure that the admissions staffs of the most selective schools, whose average SAT scores hover above 1,400, will roll their eyes when they see your 1,160. You may have something the school needs—your humorous essay on making toast might have bowled them over, or your debate trophies might have impressed them. And don't forget your Uncle Irving, the custom hubcap king, who donated the new university science building.

> Don't be so sure that the admissions staffs of the most selective schools, whose average SAT scores hover above 1,400, will roll their eyes when they see your 1,160.

You may also be an ethnic minority, live in a homeless shelter, speak eight languages, or have a major role in *American Pie 3*. All those things catch the eye of selective college admissions officers, who want a diverse student body and think a campus of nothing but 1,600 SATs would be a huge bore.

It is the minority kids with relatively low SAT and ACT scores that concern Williams. One 1980s study revealed that more than 70 percent of the African American students at the University of California at Berkeley in one class failed to graduate. Their SATs were 52 points above the national average but 229 points below the Berkeley average. "It is an academic mismatch," Williams said. "You say to me, 'Mr. Williams, teach me to box.' And the first match I get for you is with Lennox Lewis. You are going to get your brains beaten out."

Now consider the other side of the argument. Christopher Hooker-Haring is the dean of admission and financial aid at Muhlenberg College, one of the small but growing number of schools that do not require SAT or ACT scores for admission. He says a two-hundred-point SAT mismatch means a student may struggle initially, not surprising because the SAT was designed to predict first-year college grades. What it does not measure, Hooker-Haring says, are qualities important in surviving that first year and all those that follow: "work ethic, determination, motivation, love of learning, grit, et cetera."

> This being America, why would we want to tell an eager youngster not to take any risks?

This being America, why would we want to tell an eager youngster not to take any risks? The most successful educators say children from difficult circumstances should be pushed harder to learn and urged to take some chances with hard courses and challenging situations. Williams may be putting too much stress on disappointing scores from just on one test.

CONSIDER THE NUMBERS, THEN GO WITH YOUR GUT

REMEMBER, THE SAT is mostly a vocabulary and arithmetic test, with a dash of algebra and geometry, that doesn't say much about a student's chances for success in life. But in some circumstances it can affect confidence, which *is* important. "It may be worth looking at what happens to self-image in competitive situations," said Pearl Kane, an associate professor at Columbia University's Teachers College.

I do not want to dismiss Williams's main point. Many highly intelligent students receive good grades in relatively easy high school courses and arrive at college unprepared for a reading list in a single course that entails a stack of books two feet high. They will continue to be victims of this bait-and-switch scheme until elementary schools give them better reading, writing, and math skills and until high schools lure them into college-level courses like Advanced Placement or International Baccalaureate.

But for students who have worked hard and think they have a shot at one of those colleges that have alumni clubs in midtown Manhattan, the problem of a low SAT or ACT score becomes more complicated. The uncertain applicant is left with a choice. A college full of valedictorians has offered admission. Does he roll the dice and hope the first year will not be too painful, or go to a less prestigious but more compatible institution?

When I have to make such difficult decisions, I always consult my viscera. Which option *feels* better? Go with your gut; if it turns out to be wrong, you can always transfer (see chapter 18 for more on this option).

LAST BUT NOT LEAST: PAYING FOR IT

A FEW CHAPTERS ago I noted that although many American adolescents complain of too much homework, two-thirds of those who go to college say that in high school they studied less than an hour a day at home.

> Myth and misinformation have made college seem more expensive for many of us than it really is.

By the same token, although college is depressingly expensive, many parents who complain about the cost do so for reasons that have little to do with the reality of our lives. We exaggerate the burden, for good reasons and bad. We hope that reminding our children of the size of the bill will make them feel guilty and less likely to spend those four years in drunken revelry. We also obsess about the money because myth and misinformation have made college seem more expensive for many of us than it really is.

I don't discount the financial pain and inconvenience. My wife and I have paid full room, board, and tuition for two college students and are about to bankroll a third. We are glad that our jobs allow us to afford it—just barely. I think the heavy financial obligation is good for our characters. We try to get at least ten years out of each car. We almost never entertain. We take very simple vacations. We spend little on clothes, which is readily apparent the minute you see us.

We tend to focus on a scary number: $40,000. That is the annual cost of tuition, room, board, and expenses at our most expensive universities. It is a terrifying statistic, higher than the average American's annual family income. But is it an accurate measure of what most families have to pay?

This is the richest country in the world, and much of that wealth has gone into financing higher education. Every American politician, banker, educator, and stockbroker understands that our culture prizes a four-year college degree more than any other investment. The feeling unites all classes, all races, all regions. A standard happy ending on television is the troubled teenager who straightens himself out and goes off to college. Interestingly enough, Americans spend far more on fast food each year than they do on higher education, which says something about priorities and the general level of whining.

> Surveys show that Americans with college degrees earn about 50 percent more over their lifetimes than Americans with just high school diplomas.

The reason we Americans put education first is because we believe that college graduation leads to financial security and life-long happiness. Surveys show that Americans with college degrees earn about 50 percent more over their lifetimes than Americans with just high school diplomas. And that monetary difference is probably not as important, to most of us, as the professional and social respect accorded those who have at least a bachelor's degree.

What we want as a society, we are willing to pay for. The total size of the grants, scholarships, and low-interest loans available each year to college and university students has reached $74 billion. That is about $5,000 a year for every student in college or graduate school today, even though not all of them need the money.

SO WHAT DOES IT REALLY COST?

HOW MUCH DOES a college education cost, then? Most of the students attending $40,000-a-year universities do not pay that much. More than half of them, in some cases as many as 75 percent, qualify for financial aid. That includes some students from families whose annual incomes top $100,000. Surveys show that for all public colleges, from the most to the least expensive, 75 percent of students on average receive financial aid. For all private colleges, the average is 60 percent.

Most institutions of higher learning do not charge anywhere near $40,000 a year. Tuition at the majority of American colleges is below $4,000 a year. Assuming annual living expenses of about $10,000, that means the average undergraduate's family is facing an annual bill of about $14,000. That is still a lot of money, but it is only a third of what the brand-name schools that get all the publicity will cost. Indeed, only 6 percent of college students attend schools with total costs in the $35,000 to $40,000 range.

When Americans were asked to estimate the cost of a year's in-state tuition at a four-year public university, their responses averaged out at $9,694 a year. The actual average for that year was $2,848.

Well, you say, everybody knows that. Guess again. A 1998 survey by the American Council on Education showed that when Americans were asked to estimate the cost of a year's in-state tuition at a four-year public university, their responses averaged out at $9,694 a year. The actual average for that year was $2,848, less than a third of what the average consumer thought he or she would have to pay.

There is "a great deal of anxiety, a great deal of fear and a great deal of exaggeration of the barriers" to higher education, said Stanley O. Ikenberry, former president of the American Council on Education. To help families see past the myth of unaffordability, the council helped organize the Coalition of America's Colleges and Universities. With the U.S. Education Department, it set up a toll-free number (800-433-3243) and a Website (www.CollegeIsPossible .org) to give families the data and contacts they need to get money for college.

Unjustifiable feelings of helplessness in the face of college costs can do harm. Parents set the tone for college discussions. If they have gotten the impression, from exaggerated news stories or misinformed relatives or ignorant neighbors, that they cannot afford to send their child to college, they are much less likely to make that a family goal. A child who is not encouraged to think about college is much less likely to take the most difficult courses and develop the high expectations that colleges look for. Saying that a child can't go to college because his parents are too poor is, then, a terrible self-fulfilling lie.

Each year college financial aid officials look for ambitious applicants who have the grades but not the money to attend their schools. They don't find nearly as many of them as they would like, in many cases because low-income students with the ability to handle college have been discouraged from an early age. Minority parents are less likely to be college educated and to know how to finance a college dream. The American Council on Education survey found that African Americans were 83 percent more likely than non-Hispanic whites to think college was not affordable, and Hispanics were 79 percent more likely than non-Hispanic whites to hold such beliefs.

Much of this book is about the angst of students denied a chance to attend their first-choice college. Keep in mind that such people are a distinct minority. The *Princeton Review* estimates that about 70 percent of college-bound high school students are accepted by the colleges at the tops of their lists.

FINANCING A COLLEGE EDUCATION

SO THE REAL problem is how to pay for it. As we have seen, that is not nearly as difficult as most people imagine.

The intricacies of financing college take some time to master, but excellent books are available at the library or your local bookstore. Two of my favorites are the Princeton Review's *Paying for College Without Going Broke* by Kalman A. Chany with Geoff Martz (2002), and Kaplan's *Conquer the Cost of College* by Elizabeth Cote (2001). These are their most important points:

1. **Price tags are deceptive.** The listed cost of tuition, room, and board on an individual college's Website is not a very good guide to how much you are really going to pay. The kind of student you have, the eagerness of the college to get her, and your level of knowledge about how to finance college have an enormous impact on how much money is going to come out of your pocket.

POINTS TO REMEMBER ABOUT PAYING FOR COLLEGE

✦ Price tags are deceptive. Be sure you investigate all sources of information.

✦ Knowledge is money. Doing your homework may save you big bucks.

✦ Pick a financial safety school, an acceptable back-up choice just in case.

✦ There is a lot of money out there; aid and/or scholarships may be a possibility.

✦ A little work won't hurt your student; a part-time job may actually enhance her college experience as well as help with the bill.

2. **Knowledge is money.** I know I mentioned this in point 1, but it is important enough to say twice. If you read either or both of the books just mentioned, you are likely to save yourself a lot of money. Paying for college has many aspects of a Middle Eastern bazaar, and once you understand how it works, you are likely to avoid wasting some serious dollars.

3. **Pick a financial safety school.** You will likely find a way to afford sending your child to whatever college he wants, but play it safe anyway. Make sure there is at least one school on his list that he likes and you know you can afford.

4. **Cheer up: There is a lot of money out there.** I know, I already told you that. But it's worth a reminder.

5. **A little work is good for students.** There are many ways for your children to help pay for their education and deepen their college experience by doing so. Not only do part-time jobs give them a sense of the seriousness of their studies, but there is a chance such work also will give them a head-start on their careers.

> This is not an investment for monetary return but a contribution to a young life, someone dear to us, of whom we can be proud for the rest of our lives.

Even we most sensible and careful of parents, having seen how we can handle the finances without too much pain, may not give up our prerogatives. We want to act like martyrs, bemoan our fate, predict financial ruin, and beg for sympathy when the tuition and dorm bills arrive. But even if we are working overtime and cutting back on our most expensive pastimes, we know deep in our hearts that we are having the time of our lives. This is not an investment for monetary return but a contribution to a young life, someone dear to us, of whom we can be proud for the rest of our lives. No big score on Wall Street can ever match it.

We know that, even if you will never catch us admitting it.

7

FINDING THE RIGHT FIT

The Importance of Life
Outside the Classroom

WHEN I THINK of college, most of the images in my head have nothing to do with classes: I am munching an ice cream sandwich from the machine in the student newspaper office at 2 A.M. I am dozing on a couch in that same office at 10 A.M. I am hammering out a story for the paper on a decrepit typewriter at 5 P.M. I am kissing the managing editor in her office at 9 P.M.

The memories of actually getting the education for which the faculty eventually, perhaps grudgingly, gave me a bachelor's degree are much less pleasant. I remember getting a D in Chinese one term when I didn't go to class very often (guess where I was). I remember falling asleep in Philosophy 1b. I remember wondering why my literature professor insisted on pronouncing the name of Cervantes's hero "Don Quick-zot." I remember sitting with five hundred other undergraduates in Economics 1, listening to a lecture that made absolutely no sense to me.

> The answer to the really important question—"Am I likely to be happy there?"—is not readily available.

We all have different memories of college. We try to pass them on to our children. You would think there would be a way to sum up our impressions. We could measure the relative quality of the experiences provided by different universities by asking graduates to fill out satisfaction surveys.

Some people have begun to try that, but the results have been uneven. We know which colleges attract the most 1,600 SAT scorers. We know which have the most generous alumni. We know about numbers of Nobel laureates on the faculty and national championship banners in the gym and percentages of applicants who don't get in. But the answer to the really important question— "Am I likely to be happy there?"—is not readily available. (For a list of not-so-easy questions to help you and your parents with your college search, see appendix A.)

DISCOVERING LIFE ON THE EDGE—OF CAMPUS

AS IT TURNS out, I found my life's calling on a college campus— well, a half block *off* the campus, to be exact. When it became clear to me that I was too impatient and too impolite to be a diplomat, I began to explore the possibility of a career in journalism.

My father had been a reporter at the beginning of his career, before he got a job translating into English the scientific gibberish at the Naval Radiological Defense Laboratory at Hunter's Point in San Francisco. Wandering around Harvard one day, wondering whether it were really the place for me, I saw an appeal for students to join the college newspaper, the *Crimson*.

Until that point, I had not been aware that some off-campus activities were so demanding and exciting that they could consume an undergraduate's life. I was vaguely aware that football and basketball players practiced a lot. It did not occur to me that there were several other extracurricular activities at college that might become much more than a few lines on one's resume.

It turns out such ventures are crucial to a college experience. I will tell you about mine, only to point out that all that you read about classes and professors and majors in the college guides may become mostly background noise if something on the *edge* of campus, not really academic at all, captures your heart.

> Extracurricular ventures are crucial to a college experience.

At the candidates' night I attended at the little brick *Crimson* building in late September, an editor named Andy Beyer spoke to about a dozen students crowded into the dingy office of the newspaper's editorial chairman. Beyer (later to become the very popular horse-racing columnist at the *Washington Post*) was one of the scariest college students I had ever met. He was tall and slender and appeared—from his matted hair and disheveled clothing—not to have bathed or slept for some time. He spoke in an odd way. Some of his vowels stretched out unexpectedly.

But his message was clear: If we were serious about the *Crimson,* we had to devote every waking hour outside class to its needs. Candidates, what the *Crimson* called new recruits, appeared each day in the newsroom at 2 P.M. They fetched sandwiches, answered the telephones, did research, and occasionally, if they were very conscientious, wrote stories that might appear in the paper. We were told that candidates were not allowed to leave the building before 2 A.M. Sleep was not important. Preparing for class was not important. I concluded if I did everything Beyer described, within a few weeks I would look just like him.

Yet I decided to try it anyway. I bought roast beef sandwiches and thin milk shakes at Elsie's, the popular diner of that era, and brought them back to the staff. I wrote stories that were ripped apart by editors, some of them younger than I was. I got by on four or five hours of sleep a night. My meals were provided by the Coke and ice cream sandwich vending machines in the front hall of the newspaper's small building.

Most important, during my three years in that grimy little world, I became an editor and found myself spending more time at the *Crimson* than anywhere else. I fell in love with the woman I would marry, made several other lifelong friendships, and developed enough rudimentary reporting and writing skills to survive the next several decades as a working journalist.

OPPORTUNITIES FOR EDUCATION AND SELF-DISCOVERY

MANY OTHER PEOPLE experienced college just as I did, reading their class assignments when they could but devoting most of their time to a campus pastime. John Lithgow, the stage, screen, and television actor, was in my class at Harvard. He spent most of his time at the Loeb Drama Center. Bernard Beale, who later created his own municipal bond firm in Manhattan, used his years at Carleton College to create commercial ventures on campus, putting himself in frequent trouble with the dean of students.

Some of our most talented politicians began their careers by organizing student campaigns and debating the issues deep into the night in their dorm rooms. Some of our finest musicians hung around the practice rooms on campus, trying out their own compositions and playing clubs on the weekends. Several television comedies are written by alumni of college humor magazines.

For his book *Making the Most of College* (Harvard University Press, 2001), Harvard education professor Richard J. Light organized interviews of more than 1,600 undergraduates on what had been their deepest college experiences.

> I assumed that the most important and academic learning goes
> on inside the classroom, while outside activities provide a useful

but modest supplement. The evidence shows that the opposite is true: Learning outside of classes, especially in residential settings and extracurricular activities such as the arts, is vital. When we asked students to think of a specific, critical incident or moment that had changed them profoundly, four-fifths of them chose a situation or event outside of the classroom.

When my daughter Katie began to look at schools, I urged her to check out the extracurriculars. This is hard for a high school student to do intelligently, because interests often shift at that age. If you judged me by my high school activities, you might have expected me to spend my college days playing tennis and running for student office. In college, my tennis game turned out not to be nearly good enough, and student politics suddenly seemed to me the worst kind of wheel spinning.

So you need to be open to surprises. For that reason I think it is risky, unless a student is very sure of what he wants or very uncomfortable on a large campus, to go to a small school. Big schools have so much going on that it is almost impossible to avoid being confronted by all of your potential futures. Business? Dancing? Metaphysics? Pottery? It is all there; you just have to know how and where to look for it.

I would have found my love for reporting at any university that was large enough to support a daily newspaper. Many of my colleagues at the *Washington Post,* including most of the editors who tell me what to do, learned journalism at big state schools that had that critical large mass of activity and opportunity. And that goes for just about every other endeavor I can think of.

So look at the course catalog of every school that appeals to you. Tell the alumni interviewer that you think the quality of the faculty is superb. Buy all the textbooks and try to go to the lectures. But be ready for something that might be only a brief

> It is risky, unless a student is very sure of what he wants or very uncomfortable on a large campus, to go to a small school.

LOOKING OUTSIDE THE CATALOG: OFF-CAMPUS ACTIVITIES TO CONSIDER

While it is impossible to list all the various opportunities and activities you will find on college campuses, here are a few that may encourage you to look outside the academic catalog when selecting a college:

✦ Athletic programs: nationally recognized football, basketball, baseball, or other programs

✦ Intramural athletics: programs for recreational student athletes

✦ Art, drama, or music facilities and faculty that appeal to a specific interest

✦ Opportunities for political involvement

✦ Fraternities, sororities, or other social activities

✦ Publications that welcome student involvement

✦ Multicultural opportunities and the presence of students from different parts of the world

✦ Interesting clubs and organizations

✦ Facilities such as research libraries, presidential libraries, or other special collections

mention on one page of the Website but will become, when you get close to it, your life.

MAKING THE FINAL DECISION: WHAT INFORMATION DO YOU NEED?

IT MAY NOT be possible to get enough information about which college to attend or, at least, enough of the information you truly want. As we have seen, it can be difficult to assess the nonacademic elements of a university or college—and those elements may prove to be the ones that matter most to you. Unfortunately, some academic information that may be crucially important is also difficult to locate.

The *Washington Monthly* reported that of fifty randomly selected research university Websites, only 12 percent clearly posted the six-year graduation rate, which it called "the most basic statistical measure of effectiveness." The article said, "Even fewer offered information about student satisfaction with teaching. Without solid information on what they will learn, students must make choices based on geography, particular programs or reputation." In 1997, fewer than 10 percent of the member schools of the New England Association of Schools and Colleges (the regional accreditation agency for more than two hundred colleges and universities in New England) reported assessing student learning and using the results to improve teaching.

But there is hope. Alexander Astin, director of UCLA's Higher Education Research Institute (www.gseis.ucla.edu/heri/heri.html), has been doing complicated work on student satisfaction. Noel-Levitz, a Midwest research firm, has established national norms for college satisfaction surveys.

We need more such efforts. Like the millions of high school students planning their campus visits each spring, I made my college decisions based on first impressions, guidebooks, mailings, and neighborhood chatter, much of it woefully distorted if not outright wrong. That was a different era. A high school senior today who applied to just two colleges, as I did, would be recommended for psychological counseling.

These days, admissions experts advise that students consider applying early decision or early action to their first-choice school, if they have one, and to at least six other schools. They should choose two schools where they are sure to be accepted, two where their chances are slim, and two in the middle as part of the regular admissions process.

> Admissions experts advise that students consider applying early decision or early action to their first-choice school, if they have one, and to at least six other schools.

Students today are drowning in options and information, with multilinked Websites for even Bible colleges with a mere three hundred students. But having observed carefully my daughter's college search, I don't think the quality or relevance of the information has improved all that much.

Teenagers, just as excitable and distracted as I was, are making up their minds based on the friendliness of the college tour guide, the leafiness of the campus, the color quality of the brochure, and the latest biases spread by their friends. The *U.S. News* rankings, as well as the other published guides, try to say something about the quality of the teaching and the vibrancy of life at each school, but, as we have seen, those factors are difficult to quantify. Overnight stays are helpful but hard to compare.

What we need is a time machine, so that your twenty-one-year-old self can come back and tell your seventeen-year-old self what is true and what is irrelevant. The wormhole physicists haven't worked out the equations yet, so kids continue to guess.

FINDING THE FACTS YOU NEED

INTO THIS INFORMATIONAL abyss steps "Nessie," the acronym for the National Survey of Student Engagement (NSSE). It was launched in 1999 to counter the *U.S. News* rankings, an act akin to unleashing Mothra to kill Godzilla, and so far about as successful.

Many colleges, particularly those not at the top of the *U.S. News* list, wanted to dramatize the good teaching and close faculty–student contacts that the magazine's ranking system largely ignores.

SMALL SCHOOL, BIG BENEFITS

I ended up attending Susquehanna University in Selinsgrove, Pennsylvania. This is a very small school, 1,200 students when I attended, in a rural area, and I had hoped to attend a large school in an urban area. But after adjusting to rural America, I loved the fun I had with my great friends, the small classes, easy access to my professors and the activities available to me. . . .

My current work is directly related to my days at Susquehanna. I had a favorite women's literature professor who told me about a local domestic violence shelter that needed volunteers. I became a volunteer there and subsequently completed my required internship for my sociology degree there. It was during this time that I decided to work on domestic violence issues as a career. . . . Now I am an attorney. I work for the American Bar Association Commission on Domestic Violence and work on projects whereby we train lawyers and others within the legal system on the legal issues facing domestic violence issues.

—HEATHER MAHER

With money from the Pew Charitable Trusts, they created Nessie. The survey has asked 286,864 students at 617 colleges and universities how much they prepared for class, how much they read, how often they collaborated with faculty on research, and many other questions. George D. Kuh, the director of the NSSE project, said only one of the program's three major objectives, use of student engagement data to measure college quality, relates to concern about the *U.S. News* ratings. He said the two others are more important: improving higher education institutions and learning more about effective educational practices.

In a less anxious world, the resulting ratings would be publicized and college applicants would have a new resource for comparing

schools. But Nessie's handlers, based at Indiana University (www.iub
.edu/~nsse), had to promise that each college could keep its individual ratings secret. So far only about one hundred schools have had
the nerve to expose their survey ratings, blemishes and all. Even
George Mason University in Fairfax, Virginia, praised by the *Washington Monthly* for going public with its ratings,
does not make it easy. You must go to
www.gmu.edu and click on "Resources for Fac-
ulty/Staff" and then "Institutional Assessment
Office." I never would have found the faint trail
without the help of the university's kind and
apologetic director of institutional assessment,
Karen Gentemann.

> Each year we learn more about how well colleges educate their students, and that can only help families immersed in the application process.

That is better than nothing. Each year we
learn more about how well colleges educate their
students, and that can only help families immersed in the application process. Maybe Nessie
will also come up with a way for old grads like me to be asked about
our memories, too, and add our views to what is known about what
works best at each school.

I am ready to fill out their forms. I will try to be fair and complete, at least as much as my dying brain cells will let me. But I hope
they do not probe too deeply into what happened in the managing
editor's office. She eventually married me and has told me to keep
my mouth shut.

8

THE FUN BEGINS

*How to Survive the Application Process
with Your Family Intact*

JODIE LANDON FELT miserable. She wanted to go to Grambling University, but her father was insisting on Cornell. According to Jodie's father, Grambling was not good enough for the upwardly mobile Landons. Jodie's friends Daria and Jane and many other students at Lawndale High were having similar struggles with their families about college. Their senior year was full of rage and ill will.

As I watched these adolescent dramas work themselves out, I was thankful I had overcome my old-guy distaste for MTV. If you haven't yet figured it out (or if you happen not to be a regular viewer), Jodie, Daria, and Jane are denizens of the cartoon series Daria, which completed its five-year run on MTV with a movie-length episode, "Is It College Yet?" The troubles of acerbic nerd Daria, her artist friend Jane, valedictorian Jodie, and all the other characters may be satire, but the last episode nicely summed up the pain and confusion that many families feel these days.

The conversations may begin agreeably enough. Should you take an SAT or ACT prep course? When should we visit campuses? How about Dad's college—or Mom's? Don't you have to study for your chemistry final? Are you sure you have time for the movies when your application is due?

Inevitably, the student winds up shouting, "It's my life!" and slamming the door to her room.

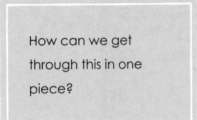

How can we get through this in one piece?

This book explores many important issues—why more students are applying early, why the SAT is a bad but useful test, why college tours are no fun, why college reputations defy reality. And we are about to take a look at the actual process of applying to the colleges of your choice and what happens after that. But as Daria seems to prove, there is one particularly important aspect of the admissions process issue that people care most about and that we must talk about before we go any further: How can we get through this in one piece?

A TIME FOR STRONG EMOTIONS

IT IS DIFFICULT to exaggerate the power of such feelings. When our children first approached college age, my wife and I were astonished at the number of families spending hundreds, sometimes thousands, of dollars on private college admissions counselors. Their children were attending very good high schools. Why reject the experienced and successful college experts on the school guidance staffs? Because, one mother explained to my wife, "We want our family to come out of this intact, and this way I know I can count on someone else yelling at my son when he hasn't finished his applications."

I have learned something about surviving the process as a family. You should expect each child, and each parent, to handle the stress in his or her own way. Our older son was annoyingly self-sufficient. He let my wife type his essays on the college application sheet. But he made all the decisions, met his deadlines, and told us to butt out.

The younger boy required a bit more, uh, guidance. We had to remind him a few times about application dates. And we did ask him (without success) to reconsider choosing Howard Stern as the subject of a required essay on the most intellectually challenging person he knew.

Maybe we were too intrusive. Maybe not. By some measures, we were models of restraint. Heather McDonnell, a recent graduate of George Washington University, told me she knew students who "were completely under their parents' thumb. It was the parents who decided where the student was applying, where they would attend school, and whether they chose early decision." She said when those students reached college they were often depressed and lost.

> You should expect each child, and each parent, to handle the stress in his or her own way.

I sympathize with parents who go too far in helping their children apply. In this culture, in this country, college is important. I met my wife in college. I learned my trade in college. Most of my closest friends date from my college days. I wanted my children to have the same life-defining experiences I had, at a place that would challenge and enthrall them. It took me a while to realize that their views on the matter should have more weight than mine.

Now I see myself as wondrously evolved, caring but not controlling, informative but not demanding. This fantasy sometimes goes so far that I imagine myself being quietly reflective when my youngest child tells me that she doesn't care if she misses the deadline, she isn't going to college, she has a good job watering plants, and what do I think of that? In the dream, I do nothing but nod my head wisely, confident that she will eventually grow up and make all the right choices.

Then I wake up and realize my wife would never let that application deadline pass without a major showdown. I smile at my wife, get a puzzled look in return, and go back to reading the paper.

PURSUE PASSION

I HAVE A mental health tip that may help some parents navigate the college application process. The selection process for most brand-name colleges is purposely irrational. Getting into those schools is very much like winning at bingo. But they have one consistent message that makes sense.

Every applicant, they say, should be encouraged to take an interest to its logical extreme. Colleges want kids with a passion. If your child likes lacrosse, encourage him to go to all the summer camps and practice on weekends. If she is a poet, take her to readings at the local bookstore and make sure she signs up for the school literary quarterly. If he cannot get enough of Barenaked Ladies, buy him a guitar and encourage him to write his own songs.

> Colleges want kids with a passion.

This is a sensible antidote to the notion that you have to be an all-star-straight-A-student-body-president-prom-queen. That was the role Jodie played in Daria, and it did not bring her joy. She applied to Grambling because she wanted to explore her African American roots and did not want to spend another four years being everyone's favorite minority group member.

It doesn't really matter what your passion is. As long as it is not covered by the criminal code, many colleges will be impressed if you go at it with genuine enthusiasm. A talented and hardworking basketweaver who sells her work at the flea market and has won ribbons at the county fair is going to be more impressive to Princeton—I am not making this up—than a kid who belongs to twelve clubs and works at a nursing home every other Friday.

Since grade school, my daughter Katie's passion has been softball. I have spent a lot of time at dusty diamonds around the New York and Washington areas. The summer after her sophomore year, her traveling softball team went as far as Pennsylvania and North Carolina, playing teams that seemed to me ready for the Olympics right now. Her team lost more games than it won. There were bruises and tears. But I could tell, because she never skipped practice, that softball was what she wanted to do. Each spring, as another school league season approached, her excitement was evident and had nothing to do with how this might look on her college applications.

FAMILY FEUD? NEGOTIATING THE APPLICATION PROCESS

IT REMAINS TO be seen, however, how my daughter, my wife, and I will handle the most irritating parts of the application process. Parents much cleverer than I am have been giving me tips.

When Ashley Doherty of Washington, D.C., had trouble persuading her daughter Dorothy Fortenberry to trim her list of eighteen prospective schools, the mother's desperation led to an intriguing solution. She got out eighteen index cards and wrote the name of one school on each card. Then she shuffled the deck and slapped the first two cards down in front of her startled daughter.

"If there was a gun to your head right now," she said to the girl, "and you had to decide, which of these two schools—on the basis of what you know today—would you rather go to?" Her daughter, intrigued, picked a card. They continued to work through the deck, pitting earlier winners against each other, until they narrowed it down to one top card and five semifinalists, ranked in order of preference.

Doherty put the list away for a few days and then brought it out again and asked her daughter whether she wished to change anything. (The mother hoped so, since all the small liberal arts colleges she had been rooting for had been eliminated.) "Nope," her daughter said. The tension between them eased, the student applied to four of those six schools and eventually enrolled at her mother's least favorite on the list, where, Doherty admits, she had "a wonderful experience."

The parental desire to check what the child has put on the application is often a sore point. In the household of Roz Jonas of Bethesda, Maryland, the rule is "Unless the kid is paying the application fee herself, then a parent gets to proofread and double-check the application before it's submitted and keep the files. I've heard too many horror stories about kids who forgot to check the early decision box on the application or who omitted legacy paperwork. If we pay, we play."

> The parental desire to check what the child has put on the application is often a sore point.

Paige Sparkman, who graduated from the Potomac School near Washington, D.C., in 2002, said her family decided the best way to handle this was to assign her younger brother the task of reading and critiquing her essays. "If he is interested, then hopefully a college admissions officer would be," she said. Her parents were only allowed to see the applications "when they were completely finished with no room for editing of any sort," she said.

Letting your kid do everything on his own will build character but may be too much of a strain for many parents. Steve Halter of Herndon, Virginia, visited several fine schools with his son and left him to do the applications with the help of his high school counselor. "When we checked with him to see how things were going, we found out he'd decided on his own to narrow the process down and waited until after some schools' application deadlines to tell us," Halter recalled. "After a small nuclear explosion, we decided we'd have to live with his choices."

He was accepted at all three schools to which he applied. He picked a small liberal arts college, made the dean's list the first semester, and is, his father admits, "happy as a clam." Now his younger brother is starting to apply, looking for a place where, he says often, "I can join a fraternity and drink beer." His father's response is "Get out the Prozac again!"

Families who managed to get through the application deadline drama without too much damage say they relied on a variety of carrots and sticks. Lisa Langdon, a recent college graduate, said her parents decreed that all applications had to be done by the third weekend in October. "I could do whatever I wanted whenever I wanted in terms of movies, the mall, TV, et cetera, as long as I got it done," she recalled. "If I didn't get it done, all those freedoms would be stripped like so much floral wallpaper—so I got it done."

Eugenia Gratto said her parents imposed a Thanksgiving deadline and banned Saturday night dates, except for the homecoming dance, until she had all her applications completed. There was also a reward, a very expensive 35mm SLR camera for Christmas, if she finished on time. "In today's materialistic society," her father said, "pure coercion is not enough."

Karen Valloch of Germantown, Maryland, said she safely navigated the application-writing process by breaking down the work into small chunks. She sat down with her daughter one Sunday night—"before the Simpsons were on," she notes—and agreed which nights the girl would work on the applications, with a great deal of time left over for what a high school senior would consider higher-priority activities.

"One night she'd fill out the easy parts of the application," Valloch said. "On another night she'd do an essay. Then do another one on a different night." They tracked her progress with colored notepaper attached by small magnets to the metal closet doors of their den. "This helped make the process more manageable for us both. Since we both had agreed on the nights, there was less nagging," Valloch said.

There are still tense moments. Sparkman said there was a loud argument after she got a disappointing deferral letter from an early decision school and bolted out of the house rather than let her mother comfort her. Holly Lown said getting applications ready for her stepson was slow torture, "and not without the kid telling us to go a few places, either," she added.

"DON'T BUG ME!"

STUDENTS WHO HAVE been through the process plead for a respite. They want all the adults with an interest in the process and a lack of other good conversation topics to reconsider asking every high school senior they meet where they are going to college. To try to suppress this most annoying of all interrogatories, Sparkman posted a note on the front door during the Christmas holidays telling visitors which schools she was applying to and declaring the subject off limits in that household. She would try not to answer the telephone whenever the caller ID said it was a relative or family friend, but her grandmother still managed to get through.

"So, where are you applying?" the grandmother asked.

Sparkman tried to be polite: "A few schools on the East Coast with good political science departments."

"Well, you know, you should apply to Emory. Your grandfather has a good friend who can get you in there."

Sparkman, biting her tongue, told her grandmother she would think about it. She wished she had added to the note on the door this piece of advice: Never tell a hardworking student that someone they don't know can get them in somewhere.

> That does not mean, several students said, that parents should not offer an opinion about which school is best.

That does not mean, several students said, that parents should not offer an opinion about which school is best. They should just be careful to use the lightest touch. Alyson Barker, for instance, was a senior at Annandale High School in Fairfax County, Virginia, when she decided she would have nothing to do with the College of William & Mary in Williamsburg, Virginia, because her parents wanted her to go there. She decided on a small, if expensive, private school in Ohio. Her parents said fine, and that seemed to be that.

"As I got up to leave the table, though, they did mention that if I wanted to study abroad, perhaps an in-state school might work a little better and that, if I went in-state, they would help me finance a study abroad program," she recalled.

They made the suggestion in such an offhand, inoffensive way that she gave it some thought. It made sense. She thought some more. Why be stubborn? She decided instead to go to William & Mary, bringing lasting peace to the household. "I always did like W&M," she told me just before going off for five months study in Australia during her junior year at the college. "I just wanted to be

HELPFUL HINTS FOR PARENTS AS THE APPLICATION PROCESS BEGINS

✦ Allow everyone—adults and students—to handle stress in their own way.

✦ Recognize that it is your child's college experience that matters, not yours (even if you are paying for it).

✦ Encourage your child to pursue her passions.

✦ Consider making an agreement (and perhaps a schedule) with your child before the process begins about when and how much you will be involved.

✦ Learn when to check in and when to butt out.

✦ Use a light touch, especially when offering advice.

✦ Take a deep breath and relax as much as you can.

rebellious and not do what my parents wanted. So perhaps they were manipulative, but whatever works, right?"

In the last Daria episode, the families resolve their issues in similarly unexpected and idiosyncratic ways. The show does not use real college names, so I am substituting what I think are their rough equivalents. Daria decides to attend what looks like Tufts after flirting with Yale, her boyfriend's destination. Jane heads off for the School of the Museum of Fine Arts in Boston. Jodie's parents eventually see the worth of their daughter's preference for Grambling. If children's choices "will help them progress toward being a successful human being," said series creator Glenn Eichler, who had a son in high school, "then you need to take a deep breath and back off."

I agree. If we parents try hard, we can get through this and still be on speaking terms with our eager and excited new college freshman. That may prove particularly useful if we need to express ourselves about the boy she brings home for Thanksgiving.

9

ESSAYS, DIRECTIONS, AND OTHER DETAILS

Filling Out the Application

ONE LOVELY SPRING morning, sitting in the garden of the admissions office at Occidental College in Eagle Rock, California, I heard something disturbing about the application process in the computer era.

Admissions counselor Whitney Jenkins, a slender young woman with short hair and narrow glasses, was conducting an information session for visiting students and parents. She had been so thorough that her audience had run out of questions. What to do?

"Maybe you would like to hear some of the things that drive us wild when we read applications," she said. Her listeners perked up.

"What drives me crazy," she said, "is when we ask you to follow directions in filling out the application and you don't do so."

What could she mean? The villain, it seems, is the business resume, a computerized device that has become so common even among teenagers that it is beginning to corrupt college applications.

"The worst is in reporting extracurricular activities," Jenkins said. "If you want to provide more information, that is fine. But some students will not fill out the actual boxes in our application and instead send us a resume. If we have to spend ten minutes translating your resume into the categories on our form, that is ten minutes less quality time to consider the merits of your application."

She moved on to spelling and grammar, confirming what several admissions officers have told me. Mistakes are very common, even in the age of spell check and parents eager to proofread.

THE DEVIL IS IN THE DETAILS

A SPELLING ERROR is a small thing. Some grammatical errors, in this inexact age, are often overlooked. But if a mistake stops an admissions office application reader for even a second, it creates an impression that is hard to erase. The same goes for decorative fonts and eye-catching topography. One admissions officer expressed dismay at an essay that had been written in spiral, forcing her to rotate the page in order to read the words that swirled in steadily tightening circles, like the applicant's chances going down the drain.

> If a mistake stops an admissions office application reader for even a second, it creates an impression that is hard to erase.

It is also a mistake to fill the extracurricular activity spaces with every club, hobby, and bake sale on which you have ever spent an afternoon. Admissions officials recommend against accumulating these small credits, walk-on parts in the drama of adolescent life, if they keep you from focusing on three or four key activities. If two of those activities are especially demanding, such as running your own business, coaching a Little League team, or writing and directing your own play, that is really all you need.

College admissions officers do not give points for every activity you list. This is not Monopoly, with your chances of winning improved by every little space you purchase. Colleges want evidence that you have taken one or two interests to their logical extreme. The deeper you go, the more time you spend, the more passion you show for at least one of your activities, and the better off you are.

Two passions would be perfect, for admissions committees have gotten into the habit of defining applicants with two descriptive terms that summarize their greatest strengths. One applicant is called the poet quarterback. Another is the carpenter debater. A third is the dress-designing science fair winner. If you have two activities strong enough to label yourself in that way, you are in good shape.

> Admissions committees have gotten into the habit of defining applicants with two descriptive terms that summarize their greatest strengths.

But you have to tell the truth. There is a temptation, as you review your life outside the classroom, to exaggerate, just a little bit. That's lying. Don't lie. It won't work.

TELL THE TRUTH

RESUME PADDING IS part of American culture, but it wears down your self-respect, a precious quality. And it will look false no matter how cleverly you package it. You may think you have a free pass to inflate your accomplishments because the admissions officer reading your file will not have the time or the inclination to check every detail. But that is because you don't understand how the process works.

If you are artificially enhancing your list of activities, you are probably doing so because you are applying to a very selective school and think you need every possible advantage. Unhappily for you, those are the colleges that pay closest attention. The person reading your file may not know you, but she will probably know at least one counselor at your school and be quick to pick up the phone to check entries that don't make sense. This is doubly true if you have a good chance of getting in, for you will likely be in competition with a high school classmate for that spot. In those circumstances, very careful comparisons will be made.

The admissions officer will call the counselor to discuss the leading applicants from your school. Which has been the most conscientious in his school duties? Which has had the best ideas and the most admirable record for working with others?

See what is coming? The admissions officer will read back to the counselor the activities you have listed on your form. Something false will not only kill your chances of getting into that college but may win you an unexpected appointment with your high school principal or your student honor committee.

THE "APPLICATION BEE"

I THINK THE best approach to checking applications is to borrow an idea from our pioneer ancestors. They used to get together for a quilting bee so that everyone could help make the best bedspread. The same method worked for putting up houses and harvesting grain.

No one can do a better job at identifying and removing unattractive bits of ego or immaturity than the people who know you best.

Wise applicants who wish to stop worrying once they have filed their applications would do well not only to follow all the instructions but circulate their applications among their friends before sending them in. Since everyone has to meet the same deadlines, why not an application bee?

Somebody offers her basement as a meeting place. Everyone chips in for pizzas and sodas. Each partygoer brings a copy of his or her application, to be passed around for everyone else to read. No one will dare pad a resume and then show it to friends. Granted, this can be embarrassing, but consider the alternative. Would you really rather leave the job just to your parents? All the spelling and grammatical errors earn red check marks and maybe a few jokes. And since the purpose of an application is to convince the college that you would be a positive presence on campus, someone they would like to have around, no one can do a better job at identifying and removing unattractive bits of ego or immaturity than the people who know you best.

Then everyone can relax, rent any of a wide assortment of ridiculous campus comedies at the video store (*P.C.U.* is my favorite), enjoy the evening, and sleep very soundly.

WHOSE WORK IS IT, ANYWAY?

WHEN I WAS twelve, my school held a contest for best Halloween costume. I decided to dress my little brother like a wrapped Christmas present. It seemed original to me and had an appropriate

APPLICATION TIPS FOR STUDENTS

✦ Follow the directions—exactly. And be sure your spelling and grammar are correct. This is your first (and perhaps most important) impression.

✦ Include the activities that define who you are, not everything you've done since you were ten years old.

✦ Be truthful. Period.

✦ Let your friends (and maybe even your parents) double-check your application.

preholiday theme. My mother helped me scrounge a large cardboard box from behind the supermarket. I got some colored paper for wrapping and cut out other sheets to make what looked like a big red ribbon. My mother helped me paste it up. My brother slipped it over his head and gamely paraded up and down the school stage when it was time for the contest.

The teacher in charge admired everyone's work, then asked whether anyone had had their parents' help with their projects. I raised my hand, as did several other students. The teacher asked us to leave the stage and awarded the prize to the best of those costumes that remained.

It astonishes me, but I am still angry about this. So what if my mother helped? It was my idea, and I did most of the work. I should have gotten the credit.

I think of this story every time I hear students and parents and educators debate how much involvement adults should have in those most delicate but important of all special projects, the essays on college applications.

Just Don't Touch the Paper

How much should parents help? The easy answer, at least when we are not talking about our own children, is not at all. That is also the answer that is most likely to drive the parents of the applicant crazy. Since the stated goal of this book is to prevent that, I am obliged to suggest another way.

When my son Peter attended Scarsdale High School, an assistant principal advised parents that they could help with homework as long as they never touched the paper. I liked that rule, and I think it works well in this case.

If your child asks you to mark up his draft, go ahead, but make it clear that they are only your suggestions. Proofreading should work the same way. The parent can point out a misspelling, but the applicant has to do the fixing.

I think a good essay has two qualities: It is not boring, and it portrays in a vivid way some attractive quality of the applicant.

I have spent my professional life trying to make myself look good in essay-length pieces in my newspaper, and I have learned that there are all kinds of tricks to making people like what you write. For one, *never* say anything that might be interpreted as boastful. Here is a no-no: "The hospital administrator said my work as a candy striper was so good that I should apply to medical school." This is also bad: "I hit the home run at the bottom of the last inning that won the league championship. But then I wondered, is that all there is?"

> A good essay has two qualities: It is not boring, and it portrays in a vivid way some attractive quality of the applicant.

It is much better to tell stories that reveal endearing flaws. Here are rewrites of these two examples:

"My first week working at the hospital, I wondered why I ever considered medicine as a career. The bathrooms reeked. The nurses were mean. I continually tripped over the trolleys that the older patients pushed down the aisles when they sought exercise. In one instance, I was so clumsy I almost disconnected an intravenous drip. At least I think that was what it was."

And, "After four innings on the mound, I had let in nine runs but only given up two hits. If you think that was a moral victory, think again. I had walked eight batters and hit two more. When I came to the plate with two outs in the last inning, my teammates were hoping that the opposing pitcher would take revenge on me and fire one into my ribs. They said they couldn't imagine I was going to get on base any other way."

You get the idea. Most of your application will be thick with triumphs—grades, honors, club presidencies, whatever. The essay is supposed to bare your soul. If all you reveal are more grades and honors and presidencies, you are going to be rejected for the laudable reason that no one in the admissions office wants to inflict such a dork on some unsuspecting freshman-year roommate.

One of the essays often asks you to examine some important moment in your life, something that exposes your values and your dreams for the future. That does not mean it has to be about what you want to be when you grow up. My son Joe wrote about coaching Little League, the principal pastime of his high school days, even though he knew his chances of a career in baseball were pretty small and did not figure in the story.

Keep your sentences short. Make your verbs active. Read *The Elements of Style* by Strunk and White.

And then let your friends and your parents look at what you have done. This is the way writers work. This book, for instance, will be shown to my family and a few other people whose opinion I value, as well as all the people I mention in it.

You can never get too many opinions about what you write, but remember one thing: It is your work. If someone says you should change something and you aren't sure, sleep on it and read it again in

WRITING YOUR ESSAY

- ✦ Don't boast or bore; let your soul shine through.
- ✦ Write about something you really care about.
- ✦ Use correct spelling, punctuation, and grammar. Yes, it matters here, too.
- ✦ Let others read your work, and listen to their suggestions. But do trust your instincts; be yourself.

the morning. In my experience, 75 percent of the time the critical reader is right. I have written something that is too long or too cute or too confusing. But if you still like it the next day, keep it. You don't want to be holding the rejection letter and wondering whether it might have been different if you had not cut that paragraph about the aardvark.

You want to win or lose as *you* because otherwise it is not as much fun, and that should be at least part of the reason you are doing it.

> You can never get too many opinions about what you write, but remember one thing: It is your work.

10

THE EARLY
ACCEPTANCE GAME

*L*AKYSHAUN MILLER OF Washington, D.C., should have been a hot prospect for early acceptance to many colleges. She had a 3.7 grade point average, was a splendid athlete, and had been diligent in her internship at the U.S. Department of Transportation.

But her family was not wealthy and not sophisticated about the latest trends in college applications. Her school, Cardozo High School, was in the inner city where students usually did not begin thinking about college until the senior year. They were far behind suburban high schools, where most families began college planning in the sophomore year, sometimes earlier.

Miller needed financial aid. Most colleges who accepted students in December, saving them the usual long wait until April, could not give her a firm scholarship offer until the spring. "I heard it was an advantage to apply early and let them know you really want to go to that school, but I can't do it in my situation," she said.

WHAT IS EARLY ACCEPTANCE?

THERE ARE TWO kinds of early acceptance programs. The most common is early decision, in which a student applies to one college in November, promising to attend if accepted. In December, the college tells the student whether she is in. It may also choose to defer her early application, forcing her to wait until the usual spring acceptance date, or it may reject her outright. A less common form of early acceptance is called early action, in which the student applies in November, and even if accepted in December, he is under no obligation to attend that school if he finds another one he likes better.

Many state schools also have a form of early acceptance called rolling admission. The word comes back in a few weeks, no matter when the applicant sends in the paperwork.

A majority of the most selective colleges have adopted the idea of early acceptance. Their admissions officials say the option gives students several advantages. If their first-choice schools accept them, they don't have to waste time and money applying to other colleges. It also helps applicants make clear which college is their first choice, a dating-game device that many students and admissions officers think increases the chances that college and student will be well matched.

ARE STUDENTS MISSING OUT?

IN SUBURBAN ARLINGTON, Virginia, just three miles from Miller's school in northwest Washington, Jeff Pyatt celebrated his early acceptance to the University of Pennsylvania by dropping his Advanced Placement government class. The course had been a painful experience, with piles of homework and a teacher he could not stand. For an A student like Pyatt at a school like Yorktown High School, the December letter of acceptance meant not only that he had gotten into his first-choice school but that he could safely en-roll in an easier government class because he no longer needed to look like an academic superstar. "Penn doesn't accept AP credit for government," Jeff told me, "and I really didn't like the class at all."

Many other high school students across the country, like Pyatt, are taking advantage of colleges' early acceptance programs to reduce their class workload and settle for lower grades in their senior year. As a result, seniors are often missing out on lessons designed to help prepare them for college. Such sloth, as well as the glaring difference in the way early acceptance affects affluent and not-so-affluent students, has produced a backlash against the practice. Many high school coun-selors, and even some university leaders such as Yale University president Richard C. Levin, have asked for a return to the days when seniors had until January to submit their applications and everybody got the word in early April. Yale, Stan-ford, the University of North Carolina–Chapel Hill, and a few other schools have gone so far as to announce the end of their early decision programs, but so far, most schools have stuck with the status quo.

> Seniors are often miss-ing out on lessons de-signed to help prepare them for college.

The overall early acceptance numbers do not seem extreme. In 2000 about 1.2 million freshmen enrolled in one of the nation's 1,768 four-year colleges. Of these, only 163,004, or 14 percent, had applied for early acceptance. Only 464 colleges, or 26 percent of the total number of four-year schools, had such programs, according to a College Board survey.

But in the most sought-after colleges, early acceptance carries much more weight. Harvard usually takes at least half, and some-times a bit more, of its freshmen class from those students applying early. The College Board found forty-one schools—all of them very selective—where the percentage of freshmen selected early was 30 percent or higher.

Penny Oberg, the guidance director at Greeley High School in Chappaqua, New York, said about half the seniors at her high-performing, affluent school (Bill and Hillary Clinton have a house in Chappaqua) apply to college early, compared with about 20 percent a decade ago. The problem, she said, is that some of these students don't really have a strong first choice among colleges. They are picking a school early because they fear if they do not do so, they will have no chance of getting into what they consider a good school in what is called the "regular pool"—the group of students who apply in January and expect to hear in April.

> Students are taking a big risk when they pick a college early just to improve their odds.

Oberg said she thinks students are taking a big risk when they pick a college early just to improve their odds. They can still suffer the blow of an early rejection. In this case, they could almost be turned down twice by the same school—a deferral at Christmas followed by a rejection at Easter. And if they are admitted early decision, they are committed to a school that may not look so good to them by spring. Cynthia P. Meade, the director of student services at Langley High School in Fairfax County, Virginia, said there "is a such a change in many seniors between September and April. A student might pick a school and be admitted early and then in April visit the campus and say, 'My goodness, how did I let this happen? This isn't want I wanted at all.'"

WHO BENEFITS FROM EARLY DECISION?

MANY CRITICS SAY that early acceptance, particularly binding early decision, is a thoughtless scheme to pressure adolescents into too-early decisions so that the colleges can guarantee high yield rates—the percentage of students who accept offers of admission.

High yields make colleges look good on college-rating lists, such as *U.S. News & World Report*'s "America's Best Colleges," and leave the impression that the most accomplished students want to go there.

Two friends of mine have written angry pieces about this. Robert J. Samuelson is a *Newsweek* columnist and, like me, the father of a college applicant. James Fallows, an author and frequent contributor to the *Atlantic Monthly*, has two sons who have already gone through the process, but he, like Samuelson, has seen enough of the early decision option to conclude that he doesn't like it. Fallows calls it "a racket." Samuelson fumes whenever he hears college admissions officers say the early acceptance option helps the most focused applicants without hurting those who need more time to make a decision.

> Many critics say that early acceptance, particularly binding early decision, is a thoughtless scheme to pressure adolescents into too-early decisions.

In a 2002 *Washington Post* column, Samuelson noted that a study of fourteen of the most selective colleges by researchers at Harvard found that applying early gave students a significant advantage, equal to a hundred-point jump in their SAT scores. A few selective schools admit this. Lee Stetson, dean of admissions at the University of Pennsylvania, has been alone among Ivy League administrators in saying that early applicants have an advantage and that he likes it that way. "The majority of students on campus at Penn are here because it's their first choice—that changes the tone of the campus," he told Samuelson.

But the apparent refusal of other colleges to admit the truth drives Samuelson crazy. The contention by Harvard and other schools that applying later does not reduce odds of admission "is almost certainly false," Samuelson said, "and colleges that maintain the fiction are being misleading and even dishonest. Bad show."

"What we have," Samuelson said, "is the spectacle of some of America's most prestigious educational institutions engaged in

> Applying early gave students a significant advantage, equal to a hundred-point jump in their SAT scores.

behavior that can only be described as antisocial. They have subordinated students' interests to their own. This is hypocritical and indifferent to any larger social good. . . . Colleges might argue that they're providing something useful: an introductory course in cynicism. But no college has yet offered this defense, which would at least have the virtue of honesty."

WHAT ABOUT MINORITY AND LOW-INCOME STUDENTS?

I DON'T FEEL as strongly about the ravages of early decision, because I think the students competing for spaces in the most selective colleges where early acceptance is so important are capable of making the right strategic decisions and will be going to good colleges no matter what happens.

But I am troubled by the failure to help minority students in disadvantaged neighborhoods join the competition. It is clear that high schools with large numbers of low-income students aren't taking advantage of early decision, because of the financial aid issue, as well as other factors. In the District of Columbia, counselors at Dunbar, Coolidge, Spingarn, and Cardozo High Schools told me that no more than 5 percent of their college-bound seniors apply early. Cardozo principal Reginald C. Ballard Jr. said early application programs don't help his students, because they must wait for college financial offers so they can shop around for the best deal.

College officials admit this is a problem. For example, only 9 percent of the 1,068 African Americans who applied to Georgetown University in 1998 sought early admission, compared with 25 percent of all applicants. "The early admissions programs tend to be biased toward the more affluent and more sophisticated schools," said Charles Deacon, Georgetown's dean of admissions. "Our pool of early applicants certainly reflects that."

He and other admissions officials said they try to ensure a diverse student body by looking for good urban school candidates in the regular pool of applicants. That just proves my point: Minority candidates would do very well if they applied early because what is in many cases their non-middle-class backgrounds gives them an advantage.

Colleges say they continue to believe that early acceptance eases the application process for the students most attracted to their schools, and there are ways to address problems like financial aid. A few colleges with early decision programs—such as George Washington University and the University of Virginia—tell financial aid applicants in December roughly how much money they will receive. But most college officials say they don't make early scholarship offers because there are too many unknowns, including the amount the student will receive from federal and private grant and loan programs.

> High schools with large numbers of low-income students aren't taking advantage of early decision, because of the financial-aid issue, as well as other factors.

I wish more counselors at urban high schools were telling students such as Miller, who eventually enrolled at St. Augustine College in Raleigh, North Carolina, that they have nothing to lose by filing an early application and that it could help them in the long run. But urban school administrators say their counselors have so many student discipline, health, and emotional problems to handle that it is hard for them to keep a close eye on potential college applicants.

Urban students rarely have their SAT results ready for an early college application because they wait until their senior year to take the exam. Everything happens too late in inner-city schools. Challenging courses are introduced too late. The college search starts too late. Financial aid possibilities are explained to families too late. If urban schools and school districts harnessed the power of the early acceptance programs, telling urban counselors and families that they had to start earlier or miss the train, it might help many students who now have no intention of applying early.

Just forcing urban schools to pay for all juniors to take the PSAT test, something many suburban jurisdictions do, would unleash the college mailings on many urban families who have never encountered such a wealth of information. I have concerns about the way those mailings are written, as I explained in chapter 5, but at least they get everybody thinking about college sooner.

> Everything happens too late in inner-city schools.

AND THERE'S STILL TIME FOR A STUDY BREAK

WITH THIS APPROACH, suburban students who like the idea of getting into college early and relaxing for a few months would not be deprived of a less worrisome winter and spring. After all, they say, their parents and counselors sometimes put them in the equivalent of one of those hamster exercisers, forcing them to run frantically throughout high school to stay even with their peers. Early acceptance gives them a chance to enjoy their friends, read on their own, and thank their parents for all that effort.

If our goal is to make the college admissions process less insane, a long, happy recess after the rush of applications is not something to dismiss without more thought. "Students want to do this not because they want to get into college early but because they want the whole process to be over," said Matt Bradley, who welcomed the early option when he was a student at Yorktown High.

If that system could entice low-income students into the game before it is too late for them to participate, that might be a net plus.

The colleges may not be entirely honest about how the numbers work, but if more students of all colors and incomes get into their first-choice school and then have a few months to relax, what is the harm?

EARLY ACCEPTANCE AND THE MANIA FOR YIELD

MANY COLLEGES WANTED Steven Bowman. He was student body president, valedictorian, and a baseball and volleyball star at Balboa High School in the Panama Canal Zone. So when he told an interviewer from the University of Pennsylvania that he was thinking of going to nearby Swarthmore College instead of Penn's Wharton School, the man tried to discourage the idea.

Wharton "is like a Bentley," Bowman remembers the interviewer saying, "whereas a Swarthmore education is like a . . . what do they call those cars? Oh, yes, a Honda."

Bowman eventually rejected Wharton and Swarthmore and went to the University of Virginia. But the Wharton recruiter's hard-sell approach has become increasingly common. Applicants as strong as Bowman are being courted by colleges more intensely than ever.

> If our goal is to make the college admissions process less insane, a long, happy recess after the rush of applications is not something to dismiss without more thought.

Deacon, the Georgetown admissions dean, calls it "the mania for yield." A college's yield is the percentage of students it admits who accept the admission offer. Schools that persuade most of their admitted students to attend—Harvard leads the nation with a yield of about 80 percent—are like crowded upscale restaurants. The fact that so many elite customers want to go there makes them even more desirable.

Why Is Yield Important?

Students and parents see a college's yield not only as a sign of its popularity but also as an indicator of how selective it is. An elevated yield suggests the school is using high standards in its admissions decisions, confident that it can accept relatively few students and still fill its freshman class. Such numbers and perceptions are increasingly important as families seek data comparing one elite school to another.

> Students and parents see a college's yield not only as a sign of its popularity but also as an indicator of how selective it is.

Admissions experts say a high yield is self-reinforcing. It leads to more applications from good students in succeeding years, more alumni contributions, and higher ratings. *U.S. News & World Report,* for instance, includes yield as a factor in the magazine's college rankings. High yield can even boost a college's bond rating and save it money when it borrows to build new dorms.

To increase yield, a college must win the allegiance of its most promising applicants. The best-known strategy for doing this is early acceptance policies like those we have just examined, binding early decision and nonbinding early action. Other recruitment tactics include warm letters from alumni, get-acquainted parties, negative comments about other schools, meetings with famous faculty, and near-promises of admission that arrive long before the official notification date.

Some educators say the pursuit of higher yields for image purposes has gotten out of hand. "It has always been the case that the higher the yield, the more selective a school can be in its admissions," said Carol Wheatley, the director of admissions at the College of Wooster (Ohio). What bothers her, she said, is that "the shift has been from a desire to build a class that offers a diverse set of talents to a desire to improve numbers for the sake of numbers."

THE LIKELY LETTER

EARLY ACCEPTANCE HAS become so popular with students and so useful to colleges that many schools have launched a second round of early applications due in January and acted on by February. But early decision and early action are only the beginning of the effort to raise yield. As soon as January, many schools know of certain students they want to admit who did not apply early. One way to make those prized applicants feel wanted is to send them what admissions officers call the "likely letter." The letters, sent in January or February, tell students that although the college can't make its formal admissions decisions until late March, they should know that they are likely to be admitted.

Penn mailed 295 such letters in 2000, all of them going to athletes and high-achieving minority students. Officials at several other universities, including Columbia, Cornell, and Harvard, send likely letters to many top students, regardless of ethnicity or athletic talent.

Students acknowledge that the flattering letters can make a difference. Adam A. Sofen, who scored the maximum of 1,600 on the SAT and attended Harvard-Westlake, a private high school in North Hollywood, California, said he thought he was going to Columbia but then received a likely letter from Harvard. "Having that letter gave me a great sense of security, and I started to think about Harvard in a realistic way," said Sofen, who eventually accepted Harvard's offer.

THE PRESSURE BUILDS

COLLEGE APPLICATION FORMS usually do not ask students for the names of other schools they have applied to. Admissions officers say they are careful not to deride competing schools. But the alumni who interview applicants are another matter. The work sheet that the Harvard Club of Washington, D.C., asks Harvard applicants to fill out inquires about other schools. Alumni are free to make comparisons, and various campuses have certain perceived disadvantages that are repeated every year: Harvard is too snobbish, Yale too urban and crime-ridden, Princeton too clubby, Dartmouth too rural, and Amherst too small. When Stanford University had to close down some dormitory rooms after the 1989 Loma Prieta earthquake, competing alumni recruiters—including me—expressed concern about space and comfort at the Palo Alto, California, school.

> Admissions officers say they are careful not to deride competing schools. But the alumni who interview applicants are another matter.

Joseph A. Monte, the college counselor at Einstein High School in Montgomery County, Maryland, said the hundred or so college recruiters who visit the school's career center each year are careful not to demean competing schools. But students and parents, he said, ask about comparative data when they visit colleges or talk to alumni, and the temptation to go negative becomes hard to resist.

Sometimes visits with leading faculty are offered to students whom a university wants to enroll. Preston Lloyd said he was torn after being accepted by Virginia and Johns Hopkins University. When the Norfolk teenager visited Charlottesville, political science professor Larry J. Sabato spent twenty minutes telling him why the University of Virginia was a better fit. "After hearing Sabato's pitch," Lloyd said, "I could not rationalize the drive to Baltimore [to see Johns Hopkins]."

Many college admissions officers concede that the pursuit of higher yield sometimes seems manipulative and overdone. Many schools send commitment cards to the names on their waitlist and will only admit those who promise to accept offers of admission. Even worse, many high school counselors are convinced that some colleges wait-list students whose applications are too good, assuming they will accept offers from higher-rated universities and thus hurt the school's yield. In 2001, the admissions dean at Franklin & Marshall College admitted to the *Wall Street Journal* that he was doing exactly that—wait-listing his best applicants.

Newsweek writer Adam Rogers reported in the 2002 Kaplan-*Newsweek How to Get Into College* guide that for about $25,000 a year colleges can buy "predictive modeling" packages, like the College Board's Predictor Plus or Noel-Levitz's Forecast-Plus. They use a technique called geodemography—calculating what colleges you might like from where you live. Then the colleges buy lists of high school students who seem to fit their profile and invite them to apply, hoping to increase their yield by doing so.

> Many high school counselors are convinced that some colleges wait-list students whose applications are too good, assuming they will accept offers from higher-rated universities and thus hurt the school's yield.

All these strategies tend to make high school counselors confused and resentful. "We can no longer predict where an applicant is likely to be admitted on the basis of the usual credential standards," said Martha Phillips-Patrick, a veteran high school counselor on leave to study at the University of Maryland. "Now we have to guess what a college is guessing the actual interest level of an applicant is. This is tough, inexact, and often disingenuous work. We are forced to counsel a student how to show interest in the schools to which she applies, and yes, even to that school which is last on her choice list—especially to that school."

My family ran into this phenomenon when my daughter told the college counselor of her Washington, D.C.–based high school that she thought Pomona College, in Claremont, California, might be her first-choice school. This worried the counselor. He explained that Pomona, a very selective college, was dubious about applications from East Coast students. Even when admitted, they often decided not to go because of the distance from their families. So he smiled when we told him that Katie, as well as my wife and I, had all been born in California, that most of our relatives lived there, and that to us, it was home. That, he said, would make it much easier to sell her to Pomona because she would not be seen as a potential threat to the school's yield.

> Early acceptance students may help raise a college's yield, but they also raise the happiness quotient on campus.

Early acceptance systems have become controversial lately. Still, for students who have made up their minds, it is nice to have the process over by Christmas of senior year. And there is something to be said for a system that tells a college which of its applicants are truly in love and which are just playing the field.

Early acceptance students may help raise a college's yield, but they also raise the happiness quotient on campus. "What these students bring in terms of enthusiasm and commitment to the community truly makes a difference," said Nancy Hargrave Meislahn, dean of admissions and financial aid at Wesleyan University in Middletown, Connecticut.

So you might as well be prepared for a lot of unnerving gamesmanship in the early application process. But if you have figured out which school you like best, it is good to let them know, as in any other budding relationship.

11

FORCED MARCHES THROUGH THE QUAD

The Campus Visit

At the beginning of March in her junior year of high school, our daughter Katie gave us her criteria for touring colleges. We were happy to get the list, but we noted a wide gap between our priorities and hers. There was something on her sheet about a cute actor named James, and Starbucks, and other things that seemed . . . well, just not serious enough for us uptight tuition payers. We were picking a college, after all, not touring Universal Studios.

Still, a reluctance to get too serious too soon may be what moved my daughter to draft "Katie's Five Factors," the academic and cultural standards on which her initial review of each college and university would be based. I quote from my notes:

1. **"More corn husks than people? No."** (That made sense to me. The Mathews family lost its links to the soil generations ago. My wife is an enthusiastic gardener, but she let this go.)

2. **"The later they let me choose a major, the better."** (I was less thrilled with this, but figured, correctly, that colleges have become so loose in their definitions of what constitutes a major course of study that it really wouldn't matter. It seemed to me that even when I was an undergraduate, some of my friends were changing their majors more often than they changed their sheets. They give diplomas these days for things like pre-Columbian environmental politics and post-Clintonian lexicology, so I figured Katie would no have trouble coming up with something eventually that they could put on a diploma.)

3. **"Size: 1,200 to 6,000 students."** (Fine.)

4. **"Good access to Starbucks."** (I was under the impression that federal law required all American universities to have at least one Starbucks for every six undergraduates. That seemed to be the ratio in the university towns I had visited. This did not present a significant obstacle.)

5. **"The James Factor—If I don't see anyone on campus who looks like James Van Der Beek, I'm not going there."** (Van Der Beek is a talented and attractive young actor who plays Dawson Leery, the leading character in the WB television network's entertaining but sometimes incomprehensible tale of teen angst, *Dawson's Creek*. To say my daughter is a fan of the show is to say Barry Bonds has long ball potential. Although the James Factor would not be my criteria for a good school, colleges are often selected by young applicants for similar cosmetic features, like scenic rivers or ivy walls. I chose to accept this criterion as just another way of judging the overall campus appearance.)

There was the possibility that these requirements were Katie's idea of a joke; like most adolescents in this culture, she enjoys playing her parents for laughs. But the more I thought about it, the more I saw the wisdom of her light-hearted approach to the standard college visit. Maybe the rest of us have been taking the whole thing too seriously. This could be a way of relieving the stress of what often feels to families like a forced march from campus to campus.

PLANNING YOUR CAMPUS VISITS

THE EXPERTS ALL say there is nothing more important than a detailed look at each school. Katherine Cohen, founder of the New York–based private counseling practice IvyWise, has a fourteen-point college visit checklist in her book *The Truth About Getting In* (Hyperion, 2002). According to Cohen, you should

- ✦ visit while school is in session
- ✦ write down or record as much information as possible at the admissions office information session
- ✦ keep in touch with the person who gives the information session
- ✦ keep asking yourself whether the school meets all your needs
- ✦ track down and keep in touch with the admissions officer liable to read your application
- ✦ investigate the school's student support services
- ✦ evaluate the school's extracurricular activities
- ✦ audit a class
- ✦ interview faculty members and students
- ✦ tour a representative freshman dorm
- ✦ eat at the cafeteria
- ✦ think about your tolerance of the year-round climate
- ✦ walk or drive around the local community
- ✦ ask your parents what they think

> There is nothing more important than a detailed look at each school.

The book *America's Elite Colleges* by Dave Berry and David Hawsey (Random House, 2001) suggests that you stay overnight in a dorm, attend an athletic event or concert to assess attendance, check the office hours for students posted on faculty office doors, and visit the career center to see whether the school offers a sufficient assortment of jobs and internships.

Private school college adviser and columnist Joyce Slayton Mitchell, in her book *Winning the Heart of the College Admissions Dean* (Ten Speed Press, 2001), suggests that college visitors act like anthropologists, delving into group relations, diet, daily routines, government, architecture, clothing, and just about everything else you can think of. In his yet unpublished guide, *Spying on the College of Your Choice* writer Steven Oppenheimer recommends looking for such subtle indicators as the ideological bias of courses, the allocation of campus student funds, and the certification level of campus doctors.

> Applying to college is stressful enough without making every step in the process a clipboard-toting ordeal.

All of which make great sense if you are a very meticulous person or if you are visiting one of the top two or three schools on your list. But for the average college visit, at least to me, it seems too much. Such intense focus on detail can be so wearying that you lose sight of what remains to be done before you even have a chance of attending the school.

DON'T FORGET THE "F-WORD"

WHY ARE WE visiting these campuses, anyway? To sniff the wind, get a mental picture, sample the ambiance, collect written material, listen to the admissions office presentation, ask some questions, and have a little fun.

That's right. I said it. The f-word.

Applying to college is stressful enough without making every step in the process a clipboard-toting ordeal. The average family campus visit, after all, often occurs while the potential applicant and her parents are on *vacation,* for goodness sake. Why can't we treat the day as a pleasant excursion to an attractive, well-landscaped tourist stop full of history and interesting architecture?

I am one of those people who likes Disneyland, and a college or university is in some ways a theme park. Call it Ivyland. Seek out the

A SENSE OF BELONGING

I made my decision after one evening on campus. I had it narrowed down to two: Williams and Carleton. . . . So I visited both. Williams was nice—beautiful, friendly, and it didn't hurt that an older guy I knew and had a crush on was my informal tour guide. But I got an impression of a slight reserve, sort of a "We like you, so you can be one of us" feel. Probably completely unjustified, but for an unabashedly anti-preppie like myself, it was a little off-putting.

Then I went to Carleton (the same place I had said, two years before, "Why would I want to go to Minnesota, of all places?). I stayed with a student, who welcomed me like I was her best friend: "We can go to the Reub, or there may be a party, and there's an ultimate Frisbee game tomorrow on the Bald Spot, and . . ." We ended up just talking for five solid hours that night, and as I was calling my mom from the lounge, the lights went out, the music went up, and people just started spontaneously dancing. That was it; I decided then and there that this was the place for me. . . . So I went to Carleton and had a great time. And got a good education and all that, of course. But the important part was that I felt like I belonged, like I could actually do this and didn't have to change to fit someone else's idea of what a college student should be.

—LAURA K. MCAFEE

best, most exciting attractions. Learn what you can without crossing the line from joyful discovery to a footnoted audit report for the board of directors.

The commercial college guidebooks, after all, have the useful comparative data, which you can read at any time. Each college Website has more answers to more questions than you would ever hear during an hour with a campus tour guide, and you can be fairly sure that the Website, unlike the guide, has been monitored for accuracy.

WEIGH THE BENEFITS

IF YOU INSIST on auditing a college class during your visit, you will not be visiting during a school holiday. This means that the privilege of hearing what a college professor sounds like will cost you time in your own high school classes, unless your high school offers special holidays for college visits. Cutting school in the last semester of your junior year or the first semester of your senior year can affect grades that will have great influence on the admissions officers at that college where you thought the lecture was so stimulating.

> Why become the world's greatest expert on a college you will never see again?

And what of the waste in time and energy collecting drawers full of information on colleges that reject you? In this era of overstuffed admissions office mailboxes, it is impossible to predict which school will let you in. Why become the world's greatest expert on a college you will never see again?

I am all for careful investigation of schools. The questions asked by the experts are invaluable guides to conducting a campus visit. I have my own things to look for, however, facets of each school that my wife and I looked for when we began our tours:

1. Is the information session helpful? This standard part of the college visit is very important. I saw some sessions run by very junior staffers who did not appear to know the answers to some vital questions.

2. Does the course catalog have interesting offerings? Most parents know what their children want to study and can use the time waiting for the information session to check the catalog.

3. Are the dormitories in good shape? Maintenance is an important sign of good management. We tried to look inside a dorm at each school.

4. Does the surrounding community have much to offer? This is a matter of taste, and we had to be careful not to impose our preferences on our daughter, but it was possible to make some informed guesses about which towns she would like and which she would not.

5. Can we afford it? There are all kinds of ways to pay for college, and I don't think money should be an absolute barrier to enrolling in a good school, but the same fine education can come with widely varying price tags. Checking the cost of tuition, room, and board is essential.

CRITERIA FOR CAMPUS VISITS: THE MATHEWS LIST

✦ Is the information session helpful?

✦ Does the college offer appealing, appropriate courses?

✦ Are the dormitories in good shape?

✦ Does the surrounding community have much to offer?

✦ Can you afford it?

There are many other things families need to know. If you are applying to a school in November for binding early decision in December, then you should give it a close look in the summer or early fall. But for the majority of students who apply in the usual way, I think it is best to save the most intense investigations for April of your senior year, after you know which colleges have admitted you.

> It is best to save the most intense investigations for April of your senior year, after you know which colleges have admitted you.

By that point, it will not matter so much that you are missing some high school classes. You cannot let your last semester senior grades drop too much, because colleges will notice and sometimes withdraw their offers of acceptance. But small lapses of concentration are nothing to worry about. And many of your friends will be sneaking off to the beach anyway.

THE VISITS BEGIN

AND SO, GUIDED by Katie's light-hearted approach, we visited thirteen campuses over the course of a year, making sure the tours coincided with planned vacations, to save money and be true to our belief that checking out colleges should be fun. Our eyes were open. We tried to avoid corn. We looked for Starbucks and for James.

We got a sense of what each school had to offer without straining ourselves. And we discovered, as I suspected, that a campus visit is often like a day at a theme park, right down to television and film tie-ins. Here are some highlights.

At the University of California at Berkeley, a homeless gentleman called us a bad name as our tour walked past him in Sproul Plaza, but we saw a lecture hall that had been used in a scene from the film *Patch Adams*. The guide said Katie didn't have to declare a major until late in her junior year, and the annual parade of witches and other pagans was just coming up Telegraph Avenue as we left the campus.

STUDENT CHOICE

From the beginning, my daughter was realistic, knowing that with only okay SAT scores and coming from a large public school, she was not going to be attending Harvard. . . . Predictably, she was rejected at the East Coast schools, offered a scholarship by the "safe" school, and accepted at many of the University of California schools, including UCLA, as well as Michigan.

Luckily, she had a friend in Michigan and was able to visit this young lady and also tour the Michigan campus after acceptance. They also "hung out" in Ann Arbor—this was as much description as I got. She liked the school well enough, but did not feel the Ann Arbor community was interesting or diverse enough to suit her taste. . . .

I heartily recommend butting out and letting the student make the choice. Visiting colleges after acceptance makes the most sense. These days they all have Websites and chat sites, and it isn't necessary to do the grand tour to see what a college is like or to contact a current student to get the lowdown. You only get a very skewed view anyway, during interviews or those soul-destroying "campus tours."

It really is true that most kids will be fine at most colleges. My daughter is now entering her junior year and is absolutely entranced with UCLA, although she certainly could not have said back in her April daze that this was a first or a "must get in." . . . She is getting As, is involved in the UCLA community on many fronts, and also keeps up (somehow) a hyperactive social life.

—BETSY DORFMAN

At one school's information session, I met fellow parent Al Franken, the actor, author, and humorist, and his son and occasional *Saturday Night Live* costar, Joe Franken. At Occidental College in Los Angeles, the tour guide explained that the scene in the television series *West Wing* I had watched the night before, in which characters played by Richard Schiff and Laura Dern had a warm moment in front of a Georgetown auditorium, was actually filmed in front of Occidental's Thorne Hall, with a prop fountain stuck in the background for atmosphere.

And there was my favorite tour guide, Jon Quinn, who, in gray slacks, an untucked coral shirt, and brown sandals, showed us the University of Chicago. I found our guides usually helpful and candid, but Quinn took that several steps further. Active in drama and enthralled with the gothic buildings that dominate the Chicago campus, Quinn said of a new business school structure, "I don't think they should be allowed to build such ugly buildings." At another stop he said, "This is the Bond Chapel. Sadly it is not named after James Bond, but wouldn't that be the coolest thing in the world?"

Quinn met the TV-cinema requirement by showing us where episodes of the television drama *ER* had been filmed. He won Katie's approval by saying, "You can't go more than two buildings at the University of Chicago without running into a coffee shop." He also referred to the university's much-praised study abroad program as "a great opportunity to go on what is basically a ten-week vacation."

With his very close haircut, Quinn didn't look much like James Van Der Beek, and neither did anybody else we saw. But Katie heard an interesting story from a friend who visited Duke University. The actors on *Dawson's Creek* have gotten so deeply into their twenties that the writers have given up and graduated their characters from high school. One of the campuses used for their college scenes is Duke, not far from the show's main studio in Wilmington, North Carolina.

As Katie's friend tells the story, the Duke tour guide was leading her group past a bench on campus where she spotted a young man, blond and nice looking, who seemed lost. "Are you visiting," she said. "Would you like to join the tour?"

"Uh, no," he said. "I'm filming here. I'm James Van Der Beek. You know, *Dawson's Creek?*"

I am not sure what about this story was more appalling to Katie, that the tour guide didn't recognize the young actor destined to be the Olivier of the twenty-first century or that Duke was not on her list of possible colleges. But, as we shall soon see, she may consider transferring.

My wife and I did manage to have fun while our daughter took her first steps away from us. I think this is a good idea for all parents. There is a thrill that should be savored in seeing your children encounter these charming expanses of lawn, trees, and moldy brick. Enjoy watching them look around. They are contemplating adventures that will be, for them, far better than anything Disney could come up with.

> There is a thrill that should be savored in seeing your children encounter these charming expanses of lawn, trees, and moldy brick.

12

HOW TO SMILE THROUGH YOUR COLLEGE INTERVIEW

For twenty years, I volunteered as a Harvard-Radcliffe admissions interviewer. Applicants to the college, sometimes as many as a dozen in a year, came to my home, first in Pasadena, California, then in Scarsdale, New York, and most recently, in Bethesda, Maryland. Not many colleges require interviews, as Harvard does, but many recommend them.

The two-page "Personal Interview Report" that I filled out on each student asked me to "please choose a quiet location and give the applicant your undivided attention, providing a positive and pleasant experience." I tried to do that, talking with each of them for about an hour in my living room. Usually there were no interruptions, except when our white mixed terrier, Mickey, wandered in.

Every applicant I met was an earnest and delightful young person, but Harvard was not interested in such general descriptions. So I filled out the report that asked me to make some judgments. "Beyond the paper record of test scores and grades," the report's guide for interviewers said, "tell us your impression of the student's intellectual curiosity, tenacity, academic goals and capacity for originality and growth. Please give examples, such as the applicant's observations about courses, research, books, public issues. Does the student seem genuinely interested in academic work? Has the student made use of intellectual potential and of personal opportunities?"

> Not many colleges require interviews, as Harvard does, but many recommend them.

I was also asked to "please assess the student's major activities outside the classroom, whether based in school or in the wider community, and including paid or volunteer work, family obligations and other personal pursuits. Does he or she demonstrate ability, commitment or leadership potential that would suggest the possibility of extracurricular or athletic contributions at Harvard and Radcliffe?"

Finally, they wanted me to judge the applicant's character: "How did the candidate impress you in personal terms? In noting particular strengths and weaknesses, be as specific as possible. Can you comment on character and values as shown by attitude toward school, home, friends? Will she or he be liked and respected by roommates, House members and faculty? Are there unusual circumstances in background? How will she or he fare in our complex environment? Quotations from the applicant's comments during the interview are helpful in conveying an impression of the candidate's enthusiasm and vitality."

In addition to completing that report of five hundred to one thousand words, I had to affix numbers to the applicant's name based on Harvard's rating scale, from 1 (future Nobel laureate) to 6 (potential embezzler) scale. I usually chose numbers at the higher end (2s or 3s) to describe their academic, extracurricular, personal, and overall qualities. Then I faxed the results to Cambridge, along with e-mail copies to the volunteer supervisors of alumni interviewing and recruiting in my area.

BEWARE "BRAND-OBSESSED NONSENSE"

ONE OF THE primary themes of this book is that attending a selective college may not be as valuable or as necessary an experience as many people believe. Persons with degrees from Harvard, Yale, Princeton, and the rest, it turns out, do not rule the world.

It is very important to keep that in mind when you go into an interview with an admissions official or graduate of a brand-name school. Some guidebooks encourage the widespread view that going to an old college with a big name is the best thing that could happen to a young American. Such a feeling, although based on myth, makes already nervous applicants vulnerable to mistakes.

> Persons with degrees from Harvard, Yale, Princeton, and the rest, it turns out, do not rule the world.

Some of my favorite examples of brand-obsessed nonsense come from a 1997 book, *A Is for Admission: The Ultimate Insider's Guide to Getting Into the Ivy League and Other Top Colleges* (Warner Books, 1999) by Michele A. Hernandez, a former Dartmouth admissions officer. Not surprisingly, Hernandez assigned great value to an offer of admission from such colleges. She also put forth the notion (doing otherwise would not have been in her book's best interests) that the selection process that determines who goes to these schools is a predictable phenomenon that could be manipulated by the most astute participants.

I have a different view. I shared it with every applicant I interviewed for Harvard. My little speech went like this:

"This can be an irrational process, like being struck by lightning. Harvard and schools like it pick some applicants for reasons that elude me and reject some who I think are wonderful. You should realize that with your fine record you are going to get into a splendid college. You are lucky to be living in a country with the strongest and most open system of higher education in the world. Wherever you go, that place is going to have what you need. You just have to be ready to grab it when you get there."

Sometimes I got looks of recognition and agreement. Sometimes, I think, my words were dismissed as a back-handed way of telling the applicant he or she was not good enough. I did my best to persuade these young people that they would be much better off if they did not worry about how famous their college was.

But this remains an uphill battle. The next section describes an example of what I mean.

THE DANGERS OF HUBRIS

YOUNG PEOPLE WHO apply to selective schools may seem nervous and apprehensive, but just the act of applying means they have unusual confidence in themselves. At the very least, the fact that they have applied to such competitive schools shows that they understand how good they look in comparison to most of their classmates. Such risk taking almost always brings rewards.

> Young people who apply to selective schools may seem nervous and apprehensive, but just the act of applying means they have unusual confidence in themselves.

But these bright young people can trip over their egos if they are not careful. Hernandez's book inadvertently exposes one of the worst consequences of Ivy ambition—a feeling on the part of the applicants that they are the chosen people, smarter and worthier than even the adults they must please. Here is Hernandez's assessment of Ivy League admissions officers:

They may consist of graduate students, former teachers, spouses of professors and college staff, and career administrators. The majority of this group did not graduate from any highly selective college, let alone an Ivy League one . . . [Many] are not expert readers . . . and most of them are not scholars or intellectuals. Add to this problem the above factors and you can understand why oftentimes subtle points are overlooked even though they can be crucial to understanding a student's academic potential.

Oh my. I can only imagine what might happen if an applicant accepted this analysis as a guide for proper interview behavior. It is not a good idea to think you are smarter than other people, particularly those from whom you need a favorable report. But Hernandez can't contain herself. "What I am trying to say without shocking too much," she writes, "is that the very best of applicants will often be brighter than many of those who will be evaluating them."

> It is not a good idea to think you are smarter than other people, particularly those from whom you need a favorable report.

Say, for example, a young applicant in the middle of an interview mentions a term paper on progressive education and, trying to be helpful, says, "Maybe you haven't heard of John Dewey; he helped launched that movement." And what will an alumni interviewer think when he asks an applicant about her science fair entry and hears these words: "Well, this gets very complicated, but I will try to summarize it for you"?

These applicants don't mean to be insulting. But take that nose-in-the-air attitude, encouraged by Hernandez and others like her, add the usual teenage awkwardness, and you send signals that will hurt you when it is time for the admissions committee to make crucial judgments of character.

WHAT DO COLLEGES REALLY WANT TO KNOW ABOUT YOU?

AN INTERVIEW IS not designed to help the college decide how smart the applicant is. It is a search for personal qualities that will assure that no matter how brilliant the student's academic record, she can deal with other people and create a congenial and productive atmosphere on campus.

Whenever I called applicants to set up an interview, I told them to relax. "This is not a test," I told them. "You don't have to study for it. My goal is to make you look even better to the admissions committee than you already do on that splendid application of yours."

I wanted to find something about them that they had not included in the applications but might deepen the impression they made. For instance, I interviewed a student at South Pasadena (California) High School who had become annoyed at the predictability and caution of the student newspaper and decided, with a few friends, to start a rival paper. What they produced was very funny and very smart—an irresistible part of any college application. But this applicant did not mention it in his list of extracurricular activities.

I asked him why. He said he thought it was too undignified to bring to the attention of very distinguished colleges. I told him he was wrong, asked for some copies, and added them to his file. It turned out to be one of the things the admission officials in Cambridge liked most about him.

What kind of questions do interviewers ask? There are all kinds, but they generally focus on three personal characteristics: inquisitiveness, originality, and demeanor.

> An interview is a search for personal qualities that will assure that no matter how brilliant the student's academic record, she can deal with other people and create a congenial and productive atmosphere on campus.

Almost all interviewers will ask what you have been reading outside class and what you think about those works. They want to see whether you have the kind of mind that is naturally curious and enjoys learning more than just what your teachers demand. Outside reading does not have to be books. It can be mechanics manuals or sheet music or fashion magazines or comic books or whatever else excites you. Just be sure you can show that you read these things not just to kill time but to forge new links in a chain of inquiry that takes you deep into some interesting endeavor.

Interviewers will also ask your views on current events, or teenage culture, or even educational practices. Again, they are not testing what you know of the details of such topics but seeing whether you have any fresh ideas.

Handling such questions is tricky. You should be honest. It is impossible to be interesting if you are saying things you don't believe. Yes, there is a risk you may say something the interviewer disagrees with and chill the temperature of the room.

> Almost all interviewers will ask what you have been reading outside of class and what you think about those works.

Take the risk. The best interviewers, the ones who have influence with the admissions committee, will applaud a dissident view. Maybe you will offend an interviewer or two, but do you really want to attend a college that allows such a stiff-necked person to interview applicants? And as I said (see my speech to applicants cited earlier), you are going to get into a good school anyway, so why compromise your values to make a favorable impression on people who won't appreciate it?

SOME SUGGESTIONS TO KEEP IN MIND

THE ULTIMATE POINT of the interview is to show that you are a good person—that you are polite and interesting and have a sense of humor about yourself and the unnerving admissions process. That means you have to be, as you have undoubtedly been told several hundred times already, yourself. And that requires a strong-minded attitude about your interviewer.

Please don't take Hernandez's advice and assume you are smarter than the admissions official or alumnus/alumna. But keep in mind, in an emergency, that you may be better at handling yourself in an interview.

Some interviewers are clumsy and trivial. A few even quiz applicants, trying to see whether they are as knowledgeable as their score of 5 on the Advanced Placement chemistry exam or their summer in Honduras or their genetics laboratory internship would suggest. Some have difficulty framing a question and force long silences that make some interviewees wonder whether they are messing up.

Don't worry too much about mistakes. Do your best. And have some of your own questions, a requirement for any good interview and a great way to fill any awkward silences. Always ask the interviewer about her experiences at the college and what she thinks of the place.

> Don't be afraid to have some fun.

Most important, don't be afraid to have some fun. You can be sarcastic. You can tell jokes. You can relate personal anecdotes. One of my favorite questions was to ask an applicant to tell me everything she did the previous day, from the moment she got up until the moment she went to sleep, so I could get a sense of her family life and her personal priorities. I also asked what interests she shared with her friends and what she and her family liked to do on vacation.

If you are going to be late for an interview, just call ahead and let the interviewer know. Never be early to an interview at a private home. (I might still be combing my receding hairline, a process I hate to rush.) Dress neatly, but coat-and-tie or skirt-and-pantyhose is not necessary.

A FEW WORDS OF CAUTION

SOME INTERVIEWERS GET carried away with the power, small as it is, of participating in the application process, and sometimes say things they shouldn't. Victims of overly enthusiastic alumni or admissions officers warn potential applicants to beware of anything that sounds like a guarantee of admission to a very selective school.

Ellen Hatton was a senior at a private school in Wilmington, Delaware, when she decided to apply to Harvard. It had not been on her list of schools, but a Harvard recruiter, hearing about her strong record, sent her several encouraging letters and even took her out for a dinner.

The meal was supposed to be an interview, so the Harvard area representative could assess her strengths and weaknesses, but to her, she said, it "felt more like an acceptance chat." So she spent hours putting together her application and was more than a little peeved when she was rejected.

> Be aware of anything that sounds like a guarantee of admission to a very selective school.

And remember that interviewers can have bad days, too. If you find your interviewer's behavior inexplicable and potentially damaging to your application, call the admissions director's secretary and politely ask for another interview.

I lost my composure once in an interview. A very pleasant young man with a splendid business career ahead of him said he had not taken any Advanced Placement courses, despite the fact that his high school had one of the strongest AP programs in the country.

I am still embarrassed by my reaction to this. I told him I thought he had been poorly advised by his high school counselors. I said I did not see how anyone could expect admission to a selective college without risking at least one challenging high school course.

He was visibly upset, yet it took me a few minutes to realize that I had strayed way over the line. I was not there to set admissions criteria. My job was to find out what kind of person he was. Toward the end of the interview, I apologized and told him he still had many good choices ahead of him. I arranged for him to see another, less biased interviewer. But if God is just, the day will come when I need a

HOW TO SMILE THROUGH YOUR COLLEGE INTERVIEW

✦ Be yourself; relax, and keep your sense of humor handy.

✦ Don't assume you are smarter than your interviewer.

✦ Ask some questions of your own.

✦ Don't be afraid to have some fun.

✦ Be on time; call ahead if you're going to be late.

✦ Dress neatly.

✦ If the interviewer seems biased or behaves inexplicably, consider calling the admissions office and politely requesting another interview.

✦ Keep in mind that no one is perfect.

job, and this young man will be the senior vice president in charge of hiring.

Keep in mind that none of us is perfect. When you shake hands with your interviewer, remember that he or she is human. I have written dozens of articles (and now this book) on college admissions. Yet I screwed up, and I could do it again.

You will also commit errors in your interview. There will be questions you cannot answer and sentences you will utter that make no sense. But if you ignore all that and enjoy the conversation, as if you and the interviewer just met at your grandmother's dinner table, your interviewer is likely to encounter the best of who you are.

13

THE TRUTH ABOUT WAIT LISTS

*E*LIZABETH BROWN, A talented actor and pianist at Granville (Ohio) High School, knew that her top four college choices—Yale, Brown, Columbia, and Penn—were big names with high rejection rates. But they seemed to want her. They had sent her effusively friendly letters urging her to apply. They had invited her to meet their admissions officers coming through town.

Her scores were good—1,370 on the SAT I, 800 on the SAT II writing test and 710 on the SAT II literature test. The college officials praised after-school activities like her drama club presidency and her trip to Nicaragua to research coffee production for a local company. So when none of the four accepted her, she felt confused and lost.

Then it got worse.

Columbia had not rejected her outright but put her on its waiting list. "At least there was a glimmer of hope," she said, until she learned—not from Columbia but from me—that the school had put 1,896 applicants on its waiting list in 2000 and admitted only six of them. "Teenage minds are fragile enough that one rejection is quite a roadblock to get over," she said. "But two from the same school—that's quite cumbersome."

Garrett Hall, a senior at Paint Branch High School in Montgomery County, Maryland, had the same problem, multiplied by several more schools. First Swarthmore wait-listed him. Then Amherst, then Duke, Williams, and Dartmouth. Yet even when his first choice, Stanford, told him that it, too, would grant him only wait-list status for its class of 2006, Garrett Hall refused to let hope die. After all, he figured, they hadn't said no yet. "I wrote some really great essays, and I think they thought, 'We just can't turn this kid down,'" Hall said. "I have the feeling they want me."

ERA OF THE MONSTER WAITING LIST

THAT WAS TRUE but, in the new era of the monster waiting list, irrelevant. A generation ago, college waiting lists offered borderline applicants a fair shot at enrollment if they hung in there. Today, with many more highly qualified applicants like Hall, the lists at many selective colleges have grown so large that they are little more than a consolation prize. Hall's first-choice school, Stanford, offered a spot on its 2000 waiting list to 766 applicants—nearly one-third the number it accepted, and almost half the number of seats available in the freshman class. Only thirty-two students on the waiting list ultimately made it in. Hall failed to persuade any of the schools that wait-listed him to change their minds, so he eventually enrolled at one of the fine institutions that had already admitted him, the University of North Carolina–Chapel Hill.

Colleges say long wait lists are the only way to contend with the rising number of applications they have received in recent years. The increase has made it harder to predict how many of those accepted will ultimately enroll. The cost for students who choose to see whether they are admitted from a waiting list may be no greater than a summer of uncertainty and the $200 they may forfeit to a fallback school if they are accepted off the wait list of their first choice. Yet wait-listing is drawing criticism from many admissions counselors, who say long lists unnecessarily prolong senior-year agony for applicants with little chance of getting in.

> The lists at many selective colleges have grown so large that they are little more than a consolation prize.

"There is a basic ethical question," said Joseph Monte, the head of the guidance department at Albert Einstein High School in Montgomery County, Maryland. "The students [are] totally misinformed into thinking they have a chance when the odds are so remote."

Many high school counselors say colleges should be more honest with applicants about how large their wait lists are and how likely they are to draw from them. "That would help students in making decisions," said Linda Hutchinson, the director of counseling at Yorktown High School in Arlington, Virginia. And some students wish colleges would either eliminate their waitlists or cut them to the bone. "Either give applicants a chance or tell them to go elsewhere," said Gina Cremona, a senior at Governor Thomas Johnson High School in Frederick County, Maryland, who was wait-listed by Duke but accepted by Cornell.

HOW BIG IS THAT WAITING LIST, ANYWAY?

COLLEGES RARELY PUBLICIZE the size of their waiting lists, and some, such as Princeton, decline to reveal them at all. Many of the letters sent to students do not say how many others have been placed on the list, although many college admissions officers say they will gladly tell any applicant who calls and asks.

> Many of the letters sent to students do not say how many others have been placed on the list, although many college admissions officers say they will gladly tell any applicant who calls and asks.

I was startled by the size of some of the waiting lists, a statistic hidden deep inside the *U.S. News & World Report* Website, www.usnews.com. So were many high school guidance counselors and their students when I told them what I had found. *U.S. News* had not reported the information in its magazine, and no one I spoke to knew that being placed on a wait list had become so futile at so many schools.

The University of Virginia, for instance, sent sorry-you-just-missed-the-cut letters to a number equaling 38 percent of its admit list in 2000. Brown's waitlist equaled 48 percent of its total number of accepted students. Yale's was 44 percent; Georgetown's, 53 percent; Johns Hopkins's, 58 percent; Amherst's, 71 percent; and Middlebury's, 88 percent. But the prize for the biggest waiting list, as far as I could determine roaming the *U.S. News* Website, went to Columbia. Those 1,896 wait-list letters outnumbered its 1,749 acceptance letters, making its wait list 108 percent of its admit list.

You will not be surprised to hear that few of these students got off the list. For instance, Harvey Mudd College, a highly regarded science and engineering school in Claremont, California, accepted 582 applicants for fall 2000 and offered wait-list status to another 322, a number equaling 55 percent of its admit list. Of those, 157 asked to be put on the wait-list. How many were admitted?

Zero.

WINNING THE WAIT-LIST GAME

THAT IS BAD news for those who still hope to get out of admissions purgatory and into the school of their dreams. But most schools do admit at least a few applicants from wait lists. The odds are considerably better than the several million–to–one shots that lead many of us to invest in our state lotteries. Johns Hopkins took only one applicant off its wait list in 2000. Amherst took nobody. But Brown enrolled 193; Georgetown, 123; the University of Virginia, 65; Yale, 48; and Middlebury, 30.

Those who won the wait-list game did it much the same way. They shrugged off any bitterness over not being accepted outright. They made it clear to that college that it was still their first choice. They were informative and persistent. And they made the contacts themselves, not letting parents do their work for them.

Helen Fields said she wrote a letter to Carleton College "explaining why I'd tanked the interview"—she was nervous and new to the process—"and reemphasizing the research I'd done in high school. . . . The day after the date when everyone's supposed to make their decision, the head of admissions called me up and let me in." Phyllis Anderson's son Jay Johnston, a student at Georgetown Day School in Washington, D.C., called the dean of admissions and the head of the drama department at Vassar, and he followed up with a letter.

Vivek Chopra, then a senior at Wootton High School in Rockville, Maryland, wrote to and visited the Cornell admissions office. He asked some teachers and friends to write letters. David McDonnell's counselor told him it wouldn't do any good but he called Tufts anyway to say he was still interested. In both Chopra's and McDonnell's cases, the schools offered an option that few applicants are aware of—mid-year admission (more on that topic in chapter 14). They both agreed to enroll in January, when dropouts and transfers produced some openings. Both did well and graduated in less than four years.

> The schools offered an option that few applicants are aware of— mid-year admission.

Robert Springall, the director of admissions for the College of Agriculture and Life Sciences at Cornell, said he appreciates a letter from a wait-listed student. The best questions to ask an admissions officer, he said, are these:

+ Do you regularly use your wait list?

+ Did you use it last year?

+ Is there one wait list for the entire university, or is it divided by majors, departments, or colleges?

+ Will there be an opportunity for mid-year or transfer admission if I am not offered a place for the fall?

Robert J. Massa, the vice president for enrollment and student life at Dickinson College in Carlisle, Pennsylvania, said the best approach is "to outline why you think the college is the perfect match for you—your learning style, your style of interaction, and your educational objectives."

> Putting so many students in this uncertain category seems just short of sadism.

Those are all excellent pieces of advice. But I still cannot get over the size of the wait lists at these schools. Putting so many students in this uncertain category seems just short of sadism. Why are the admissions people offering such false hopes to so many good kids? What are they thinking?

And then I realized I knew what they are thinking. Admissions officers are very candid about their jobs. Several of them have been trying to pound this message into me for some time. Here is a composite of what they have told me is going through their heads:

We could take all the admits and the wait-listed students, toss their applications out the window, grab the first bunch we found on the lawn, admit them, and have just as strong a freshman class as we are going to have by carefully weighing everybody's grades, scores, recommendations, and activities. How can we turn down applicants this good? It is because we

lack the power to increase the size of the class by 50, or 70, or
100 percent. So we have to put many kids on the wait list.
Maybe we will find spaces for a few. The rest will at least
know they were in the running. It would be deceptive to
reject them, because they had everything we wanted.

Katharine L. Fretwell, Amherst's director of admission, summed
it up: "The wait list is the way to honor many applicants of real excellence that we do not have room for." And unlike most schools,
Amherst extends to wait-listees the courtesy of revealing, in an at-
tachment to the wait-list letter, how many of them there are.

Some colleges are trying to resist the trend toward long waiting
lists. "I worry about the student who is very passionate about attending a given institution," Steve Colee, the director of admissions at
Macalester College in St. Paul, Minnesota, told my *Washington Post*
colleague Amy Argetsinger. "It's prolonging the agony and perhaps
preventing them from reaching closure."

In that spirit, Macalester offered wait-list status to a mere 142
students in 2000, compared with the 1,807 it offered admission.
Thirty-two of those on the wait list ended up enrolling. In 2002,
however, the Macalester wait list crept up to 235. The reason: In
2001, the college ended up with too many students enrolling and so
didn't know what to expect.

Some students and parents dismiss this notion of kindly admissions officers struggling with enrollment uncertainty. They believe
wait lists are inflated in a cynical attempt to placate alumni and keep
application numbers high.

I don't think so. The long wait lists are just one of many indications that more American teenagers are taking high school seriously.
The number of students in college-level courses like Advanced
Placement and International Baccalaureate is climbing rapidly. More
students are hiring tutors, participating in sports, and doing community work. The waiting list is a way to say that a bright applicant

has all the necessary qualities and would be admitted but for the lack of room. As we have already learned, research indicates it is those personal qualities, not the particular college they attend, that brings success in life.

So I feel better about what some still think is an unnecessarily cruel part of the admissions process. If applicants get wait-listed, this is what I think their parents, teachers, and counselors should say:

> The waiting list is a way to say that a bright applicant has all the necessary qualities and would be admitted but for the lack of room.

You are lucky to be living in the golden age of American higher education. We have more first-rate universities than ever, full of talented teachers and researchers produced by the steady expansion of American academic and professional ambitions. The top two hundred or three hundred schools, including all the big state universities, are intellectual supermarkets with more offerings than even the brightest and most determined student has time for.

You are sad that you have been wait-listed for schools you really wanted. You think that means you won't be in with all the cool kids—the bright shining stars of the college admissions race. You have read the books that say all that separates the most prestigious colleges from those a few notches down the *U.S. News* list is the quality of the students.

But you already know that the wait-listed students are as good as those who get in. Your friend Freddie got into a college that wait-listed you because he is a flautist; you play the viola and this year they needed flutes. Jennie and you both had the same great grades and scores, but your mother is a lawyer and hers is a mail carrier, so she got in and you got wait-listed. The whole process, for applicants as good as you, is a roll of the dice based on factors that often have nothing to do with brains and character.

Here is the good news: Big wait lists mean many people as interesting as you are going to be showing up next fall at whatever college is fortunate enough to get you. If the quality of the students makes a college special, then the presence of all those wait-listed kids will move that campus into a higher category, with many challenging moments ahead for you and the university professors who have to keep up with you.

Perhaps *U.S. News* should start counting not only the SAT and ACT scores of the incoming freshmen at each college but how many of them have wait-list letters in their garbage cans back home. Those discarded letters are a badge of quality, as worthy as a science prize or championship banner. Those who get them should feel much better about them than they do.

HEATHER'S ADVENTURE, PART 3

Heather Dresser came home late that April day in 1997. Her high school choir—the joy of her life—had been working on a difficult program for the spring concert. The notes were still bouncing around her head when she saw the envelope on the kitchen counter.

The return address said it was from the admissions office of the University of Pennsylvania. By the shape of the envelope she discerned, with considerable surprise, that it had only one sheet of paper inside.

She had fallen for Penn. She yearned for its funky Philadelphia neighborhood, its hearty business and international studies programs, and its many *a capella* groups. Her counselor at Jefferson said she was as good as there. She had already gotten into the University of Virginia, Washington University of St. Louis, and Tufts. She assumed the acceptance letter from Penn would arrive soon.

She took a breath, shoved her mounting panic to the back of her brain, and ripped open the envelope. She read it quickly, showing little emotion. When singing, Dresser was full of fun, but most times her friends thought of her as cool and

(continues)

controlled. As she read, her shock and disappointment mounted, but she did not show it.

She had been wait-listed. The letter was full of the usual regret and polite astonishment at how competitive the admission season had been. It expressed the hope that room might be found for her, but students at her magnet high school were unusually wise in the ways of admissions offices. She knew this was just a way to ease the blow. What was she going to do?

Being placed on the waiting list of your first-choice college is like hearing that your first love wants a more open relationship. Deep down inside you know it is over, but infatuation tends to cloud the consciousness.

When a Penn recruiter visited her area to talk to juniors applying for the next year, Heather Dresser came to the meeting and patiently waited until everyone had gone before she approached the woman.

"Hi," she said. "My name is Heather Dresser, and I'm actually a senior. I was wait-listed, and I was wondering if you could help me understand why."

The woman summoned her best professional smile. "Oh, Heather. Great to see you. How are you? We wondered why you didn't apply for early decision."

Many of Heather's friends had submitted their applications in November. She told the recruiter she had not done so to avoid a clash with her parents, who had had a bad reaction both to the Penn campus and to some Penn graduates they knew.

The recruiter shook her head. If Heather had applied early, she said, she almost certainly would have gotten in. She was a strong candidate, but her failure to go for early decision "made us question your commitment to Penn."

This was really too much, Heather thought. First she was told she was not good enough for her favorite school, while less credentialed classmates got in. Then she learned she was good enough but had failed to declare her love in time.

She was sick of the whole process. She was not going to Penn. It was time to consider her other options.

14

SLIPPING IN AT
THE LAST MINUTE

Mid-Year Admissions

$\mathcal{T}$HE LONG-AWAITED letter from Virginia Tech arrived at Courtney Zahra's house in Great Falls, Virginia, in late May. The good news was that after being stuck for several weeks on the waiting list, she had gotten in. The bad news was that she could not attend Virginia Tech until January, and she would have to take classes at another college first.

There was no room for her at Virginia Tech in the fall, school officials explained, but slots would become open in the spring term because students often left the school then.

At universities as popular as Virginia Tech, there is always, as there is at the family Thanksgiving table, extra room for people who don't mind a little crowding and a little inconvenience. Colleges do not want to turn away students. Nor do they want to have empty dorm rooms and lecture hall seats after the trauma of first

Colleges do not want to turn away students. Nor do they want to have empty dorm rooms and lecture hall seats after the trauma of first semester sends some freshmen home.

semester sends some freshmen home. So they are finding many creative ways to squeeze in more newcomers.

Some universities, like Virginia Tech, have offered students admission in the winter or spring terms. Others have accepted students for the term that begins in the summer, practically dragging them off the high school graduation stage and popping them into their first college classes. Still other colleges are trying to make more room by inviting older students to move off campus, cutting back on transfer students and using product management techniques (such as sophisticated computer software), first developed in factories and supermarkets, to track courses, enrollment, and students needs.

MULTIENTRY ADMISSIONS

TRENT ANDERSON, THE vice president for publishing and e-ventures at Kaplan, Inc., the test preparation company, estimates that at least half of the four-year colleges in the country have adopted admissions systems that diverge from the normal fall enrollment.

Zahra was among two hundred students who accepted admission at Virginia Tech for January of 2001. For the fall semester, 4,700 students accepted admission. Shelley Blumenthal, the associate director of undergraduate admissions at the Blacksburg, Virginia, school, said its spring admissions policy began in 1998 as the college's popularity reached new heights. Applications poured in from strong students "to whom we would have offered [fall] admission before, but because of the competition and the increasing strength of the applicants, we had to place these students on the waiting list," he said.

Anderson and other specialists predict that the trend of so-called multientry dates for college students will grow as the number of college applicants increases through the first decade of the twenty-first century. An important factor is computer software that allows universities to keep better track of semester-by-semester fluctuations in enrollment and dormitory space.

In recent years, Colby College, in Waterville, Maine, has offered more than one hundred students each year a chance to start school in January after spending the fall term at Colby-sponsored study centers in France, Spain, or England. Harvard University decided in 1996 to cut the number of transfers it admitted from about 110 to 75 so it could accept more high school seniors. The University of Maryland has been offering spring admission to several hundred waitlisted students in recent years, and unlike Virginia Tech, it does not require them to attend another college in the fall.

> Multientry dates for college students will grow as the number of college applicants increases through the first decade of the twenty-first century.

RESCUING THE WAIT-LISTED

ONE OF THE most sophisticated approaches to rescuing the waitlisted takes place at the University of Florida at Gainesville. The school accepts new students in the fall, spring, and summer quarters. Many of those who start in the summer take breaks at other times of the year, thus easing the strain on facilities. School officials also keep a computerized inventory of which courses each student needs to graduate and when the student should take those classes. Some premed students who need organic chemistry will be told to take it in the fall, for example, while others will take it in the summer.

The new system has allowed the university to admit more students and still avoid crowding in key courses, school officials say.

University of Florida president John V. Lombardi likens it to the method factories and stores use to ensure that products arrive just when customers need them.

High school counselors have begun to embrace the new admissions systems. Bob Turba, the chairperson of guidance services at Stanton College Preparatory School, a public school in Jacksonville, Florida, said many of his students, often the first in their families to go to college, like the summer term option offered at many Florida state schools. "It is easier for them to get in, and if they take a course or two in the summer and are successful, they just move on into the fall semester," he said.

Olivia Odell, who accepted summer admission at the University of Florida, said she saw many advantages. "There are fewer people, and the classes are smaller," said Odell, who decided to major in health science education. "Summer is a terrific time to come to college and just learn where everything is."

Most colleges that admit in the spring or summer do not include those students' SAT scores—which typically are lower than the SAT scores of fall admittees—when calculating the average SAT score of the freshman class. That ensures that the college will not suffer a lower ranking in lists such as the one published by *U.S. News & World Report*. Sheldon E. Steinbach, the general counsel for the Washington-based American Council on Education, called the practice "one of our dirty little secrets."

But officials at schools that are dipping deeper into their wait lists say they are admitting students with first-rate credentials and are not lowering their standards in any way. Zahra, for example, was a yearbook editor and a strong B-plus student at Langley High, one of the most academically challenging schools in Virginia. Teachers raved about her leadership qualities and her work with hearing-impaired and developmentally disabled children. Her SAT scores were below those of other students with similarly attractive applications, but her counselor, Brian Doyle, and Langley's college and career counselor, Brenda Whalen, called and e-mailed Virginia Tech admissions officers on her behalf.

Karen Torgenson, Virginia Tech's director of undergraduate admissions, called Doyle back to tell him that she thought Zahra would be a good candidate for the expanded spring admission program. A May 27 letter told Zahra she had to enroll for the fall in an acceptable community college or four-year school and compile a grade point average of at least 2.5, with no grade less than a C. In this way, Virginia Tech officials said, their spring admittees can still count on graduating in four years.

> If placed on a wait list, a student would be wise to inquire about unconventional admission options.

Zahra certainly had other options. She had been accepted at four other colleges. But Virginia Tech had a gorgeous campus, a rapidly growing reputation for excellence, and an education training program she liked.

So she accepted the invitation to enroll late, one of the first of many college applicants who will do so in the future. "It's one of those gut feelings," she said. "I just knew that was where I wanted to go."

So if placed on a wait list, a student would be wise to inquire about unconventional admission options. Starting college in the summer or the spring may seem weird, but at least you are where you want to be, with four years to adjust.

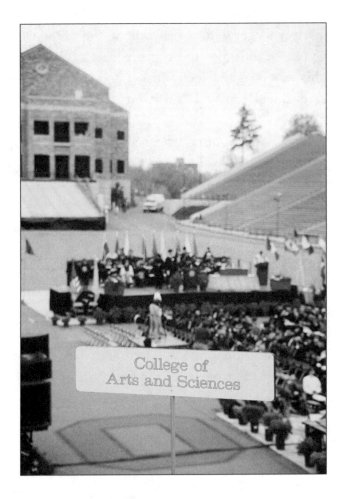

15

WHERE DO HEROES
GO TO COLLEGE?

$\mathcal{N}$O ONE WANTS to be rejected by the college of his or her choice. In fact, the dreaded rejection letter is among a high school senior's worst nightmares. But it does happen. What can you do if it happens to you?

The first few days after being rejected by your first-choice school, you fight the disappointment—sometimes your parents' as well as your own. You hear the usual responses, from friendly to passive-aggressive. You didn't get into Princeton? Well, it's their loss. Wait-listed at Stanford? Big deal. Rejected by Yale? You should have worked harder during high school.

> The dreaded rejection letter is among a high school senior's worst nightmares.

You try to be polite to well-wishers, even if they compound the hurt. But there are much better ways to move on. Consider the lessons of chapter 1. Whatever you want out of life—money, job satisfaction, love—no college, no matter how selective and special, is guaranteed to deliver it to your doorstep. In fact, it does not matter where you go to school. Now take it one significant step further.

BIG NAMES FROM NO-NAME SCHOOLS

LET'S SAY YOUR ambitions extend beyond the dreams of an ordinary person. You want to change the world. So you should ask yourself: Where did your heroes go to college?

Many of us want our years on this planet to have meaning. We want to save lives, create new things, add value to our society. In other words, we want to be admired. That is hard to do. What college do you go to for that? Where did the people you look up to get their degrees?

Well, for starters, let's examine the resumes of U.S. presidents. The College of William & Mary likes to claim Thomas Jefferson, and Harvard takes credit for the Adamses, but that was a different era—no SATs, no waiting lists, essentially open admission for anybody who could afford to sell a cow to pay the bill.

> Where did the people you look up to get their degrees?

The last three presidents have been brand-name products, the Bushes of Yale and Georgetown grad Bill Clinton. In my lifetime, we have also had two presidents from Harvard and one each from Michigan, West Point, and Annapolis. But there have also been presidents from Southwest Texas State Teachers College, Whittier College, Eureka College, and one, Harry Truman, who took some law courses but never earned a college degree. The lists of governors and senators in chapter 1 suggest that as the years pass, we will have more people in the Oval Office from schools you never heard of.

I think even the most sorrowful rejectees eventually begin to appreciate this. Whatever disappointment American adolescents feel at being stiffed by well-known colleges often evaporates when they arrive at their new schools and find them throbbing with intellectual adventures, interesting parties, and romance. They, like their parents, eventually look back and realize the people who made the biggest impact on our lives were far more likely to go to a no-name school or no school at all.

Whom do we admire? Here are six people on my list: Martin Luther King, Jaime Escalante, Katharine M. Graham, Billie Jean King, William J. Bennett, and Richard W. Riley. Nobel laureate King went to Morehouse; publisher Graham, to Vassar and the University of Chicago; and former education secretary Bennett, to Williams, all brand-name schools. But Escalante, the calculus teacher made famous by the film *Stand and Deliver,* and King, the tennis star, made do with degrees from California State University–Los Angeles. (Escalante earlier graduated from Normal Superior in La Paz, but the credits did not count in the United States.) Riley, the former South Carolina governor and education secretary, graduated from Furman University.

> Whatever disappointment American adolescents feel at being stiffed by well-known colleges often evaporates when they arrive at their new schools and find them throbbing with intellectual adventures, interesting parties, and romance.

That is just my list, a small, skewed sample. So I asked friends and relatives for their selections. Here are the names they offered, in alphabetical order. They cover a broader (to say the least) definition of heroism than I would subscribe to, but I promised not to censor them: Muhammad Ali, Karen Allen, Luis Alvarez, Warren Buffett, Ken Burns, Bill Cosby, Bob Costas, Emily Dickinson, Don DeLillo, Richard Feynman, Bill Gates, Rudy Giuliani, Lee Iacocca, Steve Jobs, Garrison Keillor, Sarah McLachlan, Bette Midler, Julia Morgan, Al Neuharth, Sarah Jessica Parker, Abe Pollin, Colin Powell, Anne Rice, Dot Richardson, Julian Simon, Ted Turner, Kevin Williamson, Oprah Winfrey, Henry Winkler, and Tiger Woods. That's thirty names. I would say ten of them attended the sort of selective schools we are talking about: software magnate Gates (Harvard), golfer Woods (Stanford), poet Dickinson (Mount Holyoke), economist Simon (Harvard), physicist Feynman (MIT), softball star Richardson (UCLA), physicist Alvarez (University of Chicago), computer magnate Jobs (Reed), architect Morgan (Berkeley), and media magnate Turner (Brown). But I find it interesting that so many of them either dropped out of college (Gates, Woods and Dickinson) or were kicked out (Turner—twice!).

Some, such as actor Parker, boxer Ali, and singer McLachlan, did not attend college. The rest went to less celebrated schools: Fashion Institute of Technology (actor Allen), Nebraska–Lincoln (tycoon Buffett), Hampshire (filmmaker Burns), Temple (comedian Cosby), Syracuse (sportscaster Costas), Fordham (novelist DeLillo), Manhattan (former mayor Giuliani), Lehigh (carmaker Iacocca), Minnesota (humorist Keillor), Hawaii (singer Midler), South Dakota (newspaper publisher Neuharth), George Washington (Washington Wizards owner Pollin), City College of New York (Secretary of State Powell), San Francisco State (novelist Rice), East Carolina (screenwriter/ producer Williamson), Tennessee State (talk-show host Winfrey), and Emerson (actor Winkler).

(Author's note: I realize that I have failed, as some friends have noted, to explore the obvious corollary to heroes who attend no-name schools—that is, identifying the many loathsome people who have attended some of our best colleges. It is a tempting suggestion. But I think I will leave that more detailed list for another day—at least until after I talk to my lawyer.)

WHERE DOES GREATNESS COME FROM?

NO ONE IS quite sure where greatness comes from. But I think we can agree that it does not have much to do with the name of the college on top of the person's diploma. See for yourself. Go to www .google.com, type in your hero's name plus the word *biography,* hit Enter, and the collegiate portion of that person's past will be revealed.

I like the way Nicholas Lemann handles this issue in his book, *The Big Test: The Secret History of the American Meritocracy* (Farrar Straus & Giroux, 2000). He calls people who go to the best-known schools the American Mandarins. They have their place in our society, mostly as technicians and consultants and skilled professionals. They are very good at discerning the rules and carrying out their assignments. The people who make a difference, who create new companies or change minds or establish trends, Lemann calls the Talents. They don't need a high SAT score, good extracurricular activities, and a dynamite application essay to make their mark.

> Be happy at your chance to spend four years at any college, soaking up the wisdom of the world and deciding what kind of life you want.

So relax. Be happy at your chance to spend four years at any college, soaking up the wisdom of the world and deciding what kind of life you want. A few of you are destined to be heroes, and the qualities that will make you so are already in your possession.

16

APRIL ANGST

Admit Weekend and
Other Tales

*L*ET'S SAY YOU'RE one of the lucky ones. You receive the longed-for letter of acceptance from the college of your choice. In fact, perhaps you're accepted by several colleges of your choice. Now what?

One of the most recent manifestations of the American fixation on college admissions is the on-campus weekend, an annual attempt—usually at the middle or end of April—to ensure that a student accepts a college's offer of admission by giving her two or three of the most thrilling, enlightening, and, in a few cases, intoxicating days she has ever experienced.

These events operate under different names. At Duke it is "Blue Devil Days." At Stanford it is "Admit Weekend." MIT calls its main April attraction "Campus Preview Weekend." Cornell goes with the simpler "Cornell Days." But they all have the same idea: Show every student who has been admitted what a cornucopia of social and educational delights await them, particularly on non–school nights when they can party.

I imagine some soon-to-be college freshmen still cherish the memories of their on-campus weekends, but is that a good thing? Are colleges spending too much time and money on these carnivals? Do they help students and their families survive what is probably the worst part of the whole college application process?

> They all have the same idea: Show every student who has been admitted what a cornucopia of social and educational delights await them, particularly on non–school nights when they can party.

THE WORST PART OF THE PROCESS

WHILE WRITING ABOUT admission misadventures, it has dawned on me that the scariest moments occur during one thirty-day period. If you are a high school senior and your nerves are shot, your energy drained, and your family deeply split, you don't have to look at the calendar. You can be pretty certain it is April.

The month begins for many seniors with the fretful wait for acceptance letters from colleges. They may have to spend several days swabbing the psychic wounds of rejection and enduring intrusive questions (and even more annoying condolences) from friends and relatives. April means anguishing over financial aid, strategizing wait lists, arguing with wrong-headed parents, and suffering smug friends who have already made up their minds. Students must keep up grades so the acceptance letters won't be revoked, and, amid all that, they must try to distill the vital essence of the colleges that did accept them, who are now showering them with urgent appeals.

Which brings me to the ticklish matter of the last-minute college visit. I recommended in chapter 11 that applicants have fun on their first college tours. Soak up the sights and collect the admissions of-

A TYPICAL WEEKEND?

I didn't attend College Preview Weekend [CPW] at MIT and instead overnighted in a fraternity house later in April and am very glad I did. It gave me a much better idea of what life up here was like—certainly more boring than if I'd come up when all the parties were going on. I got to see people working late into the night in typical MIT fashion, but I also got to see the community and friendships they had.

Now that we're bitter upperclassmen who work all the time, my friends and I joke about scaring the pre-frosh by telling them what life is really like at MIT. Invariably, the weather is always good that weekend—after five months of Boston winter—and the admissions office sets up tons of social events. Alcohol is banned, but it seems like the only weekend where people are out barbecuing and having a good time. Professors even spice up their lectures on the Friday of CPW.

Going to a preview weekend in April isn't necessarily bad—it's kind of like taking a campus tour and going to the info session. You get about 25 percent of the story. The best thing is always to talk to people at the school and see it for yourself.

—ADAM EAMES, MIT '04

fice materials, but leave the heavy work of course analysis, faculty interviews, and dorm inspections for April, when you will know which schools have accepted you.

This is fine as far as it goes, but it overlooks the difficulties of cutting through the noisy jumble of on-campus barbecues and dances and symposia. I have a fascinating account of this refined, collegiate huckstering, written in 2001 by Amy Luxenberg when she was a senior at the Thomas Jefferson High School for Science and Technology in Fairfax County, Virginia. She eventually succumbed to the allure of MIT's Campus Preview Weekend and went on to major at that university in computer science. She searched Websites and collected stories from other high school seniors, particularly those who weren't so inebriated during their visits that they couldn't recall the details. (Luxenberg told me the admit weekends she investigated had very strict rules about alcohol, and memories were very clear.)

A REVELATION OR A SHAM?

IS THE TYPICAL on-campus weekend a revelation or a sham? Luxenberg found indications of both. In the MIT newspaper the *Tech* during that school's Campus Preview Weekend in 2001, sophomore Mike Hall titled his column, "CPW: Temptation and Terror." It was a fictional journal by a student drawn to MIT by the glow of his on-campus weekend experience, only to find that the actual life of a Techster was, to put it mildly, a bit more mundane.

In the *Stanford Daily*, student Arisha Hatch said one of her dorm-mates imagined an apt headline: "Admit Weekend: The Lie Begins." She said, "House hosts began to make elaborate preparations for the upcoming weekend of endless parties and social events—which is obviously a far cry from the truth here at Stanford." Stanford's schedule of activities for Admit Weekend was twenty-two pages long. It offered campus tours; information sessions ranging from fraternity/sorority life to academic advising; an activities fair; an *a cappela* choral concert; and an assortment of parties, dorm get-togethers, and chances to speak to Stanford professors. Luxenberg said when she checked the Stanford Web calendar for a more conventional weekend in late May, long after the May 1 deadline, she found only a few academic lectures and seminars, plus a taiko festival and a beach trip.

I don't see much harm in mounting such fiestas. I don't think the universities can fairly be accused of false advertising and preying on impressionable youth. Weekends at my house are usually excruciatingly dull—grocery shopping, gardening, laundry, and if my wife and I are feeling frisky, a movie and maybe a grilled cheese sandwich and chocolate shake at the American City Diner on Connecticut Avenue. But if relatives are coming, we will try to arrange a museum visit or tickets to something at the Kennedy Center. Because colleges in April are in effect welcoming these young people to their campus family, there is nothing wrong with putting on a good show.

But the impression created by two days of fun can have a great deal of influence, coming as it does just before decision day. Luxenberg describes what happened to her Jefferson High classmate, Savanna Lyons. Lyons got into Yale and Harvard but was strongly inclined to go to the former. She was enthralled with her Yale alumni interview, where she fell naturally into a deep discussion of technologies used for drilling in the Arctic National Wildlife Refuge.

Despite her strong Yale leanings at the beginning of April, the on-campus weekends changed her mind. She told Luxenberg, "Both Harvard and Yale did a fairly good job of showcasing all their activities and performance groups. But Harvard and its student organizations offered more nighttime activities for their visitors, including an ice cream social and a few really good dance parties. Yale didn't really supply anything for us to do—the only entertainment available was a cramped and very gross beer party in someone's dorm."

> These last-minute visits can have an extraordinary effect, canceling out months of research, interviews, discussion, and thought.

Some readers will be puzzled by her choice. To them, a raucous party soaked with adult beverages is the epitome of the college experience. I also suspect that Lyons had the bad luck to miss more genteel happenings in New Haven that weekend. I offer her story only to show that these last-minute visits can have an extraordinary effect, canceling out months of research, interviews, discussion, and thought.

BIG NAME AND BIG PIZZA

When I was eighteen, the choice came down to two colleges: Columbia and Haverford. I was extremely fortunate to have the option between them, and I still believe I would have been successful and happy at either one.

But only Columbia had the Jumbo Slice.

After visiting both schools and having a great (and only marginally illicit) time at both, one thing stood out for me: At Koronet Pizza, just a few blocks down Broadway from the Columbia campus, you could buy the biggest piece of pizza I'd ever seen for $1.75.

It was good pizza, too. I should know, because I attended Columbia and had the opportunity to eat many more slices over the next four years. I live in New York now, and I never visit the old alma mater without eating either a Jumbo Slice from Koronet's (the price is now a whopping $2.50 in these troubled economic times) or a falafel from Amir's, another establishment I first visited during the application process.

Now, I'm not recommending that all high school seniors make their college decisions based on things like pizza and falafel, but I firmly believe that those decisions should be made on criteria beyond the hard "data." After all, college is not just a place to be educated; it's going to be your home for four years, and if you can't find ways to personalize your college, to make it your own, then maybe you're not in the right place.

—DAVID KONSCHNIK

Lyons, like any clearheaded graduate of a top science high school, acknowledged that there was no verifiable data to support her conclusions. She could not prove that her different weekend experiences had any relevance for the relative worth of the two cam-

puses. She made her choice—she had to go somewhere—but re-
sisted reaching any firm conclusion: "I think that if Yale had presented a better image of itself, I would have been much more likely to
go there, since I initially entered the orientation with a Yale-favoring
bias. Then again, maybe the lack of planned activities for prefrosh
and the lack of camaraderie that I felt with the other students really
was reflective of how the college was different from Harvard."

HOW INVOLVED SHOULD PARENTS BE?

I HAVE NOT said much about the most anxious participants in the
dramatic events of April senior year—the parents. Some are very
cool about it. I think I am in that category, although I am not letting
anyone who thinks otherwise come anywhere near this keyboard.

And I haven't had much of a challenge so far. My older son got
into college early action, and my younger son had no trouble selecting from among the schools that accepted him. My daughter also
applied early. If that doesn't work out and I do find myself waiting
on April 1 for her to tell me what the letters say, it will be after this
book has gone to press. You will have to locate me and ask me a lot
of questions in order to discover how I actually behaved.

But I do want to offer, as a benchmark for parents, the story of
Bob McConnaughey, who experienced a more interesting April than
most. McConnaughey and his wife, Patty Blanton, do data and statistical programming for the National Institute of Environmental
Health Sciences in Research Triangle Park, North Carolina. Their son
Adam is an only child, and an unusual one at that. His father describes him as "a skinny white boy with long orange curls interested
in math/music compositions and playing in bands." In April 2002,
while completing his senior year at the North Carolina School of Science and Mathematics, a statewide magnet school in Durham, Adam

received offers of admission from Oberlin, Grinnell, Macalester, Davidson, and the University of North Carolina–Chapel Hill. He did not, however, get into UNC's special honors program, which surprised his father.

The family visited the campuses. McConnaughey sought more detail on the admission offers. This produced a series of e-mail messages, particularly with North Carolina officials, which are so illustrative of April angst that I am going to reproduce parts of them here.

McConnaughey was much more involved than I think is healthy. In one (unsent) message, he asked, "Is Adam getting into the honors program because his dad's a pushy alumnus jerk?" Still, his messages are so candid and good-hearted and his son's record so remarkable that I found their story irresistible. Also, his principal interlocutor at North Carolina, senior associate director of admissions Stephen Farmer, revealed the vast reserves of patience and humanity that, thankfully, are often found among admissions officers these days.

April 17, 2002, 6:30 P.M.
To: Adam McConnaughey
From: UNC–Chapel Hill Admissions

As of this morning we had not yet received your reply form confirming your intention to enroll in our entering class. Please remember that the postmark deadline for your completed reply form is May 1, 2002. If you wish to accept our offer of admission and confirm your place at Carolina, your form must be completed and postmarked by that date.

If you have not yet decided where you will enroll next fall, please consider visiting Carolina, either in person or online. To register for a campus tour, please visit your UNC homepage at www.admissions.unc.edu, follow the links to the login page, and enter your username: adamcoron and password: adam123. If we can help in any way as you make plans to visit, please let us know.

April 17, 2002, 7:44 P.M.
To: UNC–Chapel Hill Admissions
From: Bob McConnaughey

We've been waiting to see, if among other things, certain portions of the UNC admissions bureaucracy will ever reply to our inquiries! Basically we were simply wondering what the criteria were for being invited into the honors program. As y'all know, Adam's SATs were 1570 (higher than the 1510/1540 in or out-of-state averages for Carolina Scholars). He had 800s on both the English and Math II c exams; he was the high scoring senior in the state this year on the AMC12a (what used to be the American High School Math Exam); five out of the six times he entered the NC Music Teachers composition contest he won—from grade school through high school, won the Southern regionals once, runner up once; oh yeah, National Merit finalist/and scholar if Adam chooses Macalester. We've written earlier to the UNC honors and scholarship program offices, without having had the courtesy of a reply yet.

We're also curious as to how bollixed the admissions process could become if a student doesn't use the "special" username/password sent to recruited applicants? I ask because there seemed to be little contact between the various arms of the admissions process. Adam received a "personal" username/password last spring, presumably because he was a National Merit semifinalist at that point. However, he applied to UNC under a different username/password. Several times after he'd completed the application, he received notes from Dr. Lucido's office asking him to be sure to apply, because the provided username hadn't been "activated." In turn, he replied, each time, saying, yes, the application *had* been completed, just using a different username. As far as we could see there was never any cross-linkage between offices/computers databases/ whatever because these pleas to apply kept coming up till Jan 29th. It would be really nice to get an honest answer to this question before Adam has to decide between accepting scholarships to Grinnell or Macalester, or going to UNC. We're not expecting a scholarship to fall out of the sky . . . but a simple answer *would* be appreciated.

April 18, 2002, 5:37 P.M.
From: Stephen Farmer
To: Bob McConnaughey

Thank you for writing about your and your son's distressing experiences with our office. I'm sorry that no one has yet responded to your previous questions about why Adam was not invited to join the honors program at Carolina. I'm also sorry about the problems he encountered as a result of his having two student records in our information system. Most of all, I'm sorry that these experiences have left him, and you, doubting our commitment to him as a student, or to undergraduate students more generally.

Adam came to us as a prospect in two ways. We purchased his name from the Student Search Service of the College Board last May, created a record for him, and contacted him by letter. In November, Adam visited our Website and created a new record for himself; the new record included a slightly different name and mailing address, and a completely different e-mail address, from those in the earlier record. These differences— especially the different e-mail address—allowed Adam to create this duplicate record without our first deleting his old one. We should have subsequently deleted the old record when Adam wrote to inform us of our misdirected e-mails, and I'm sorry that we didn't. Athough I know this will do Adam little good, I have since deleted the old record, and I will talk with our staff about our oversight and our need to improve in this area.

As for honors, we work closely with Tom Warburton, the director of the program, throughout the year in the nomination and selection of honors students. We read each freshman application carefully, with an eye toward admission both to the university and to honors. In Adam's case, while we were duly impressed by his results on standardized tests and his overall performance at science and math, we found that the decline in his grades from his junior to senior year did not make a strong case for his inclusion in the honors program as a freshman. We also found that his essays were average for our applicant pool in both content and style.

I can appreciate that our reservations probably seem small in light of Adam's larger achievements as a student and a person. In fact, in any absolute sense, these reservations are small. At the same time, the competition for spaces in our honors program is so keen that reservations such as these do often prevent us from including even very talented students such as Adam.

Despite our decision regarding the honors program, we have a high regard for Adam and for his potential for success here at Carolina. I very much hope that neither our decision nor our failure to respond quickly to your previous inquiry will lead him to conclude otherwise.

To: Stephen Farmer
From: Bob McConnaughey

I just wanted to let you know that we really appreciated getting your kind and informative note explaining the whys and wherefores of Adam's peregrinations through the UNC admissions process (which, hitherto, had been quite mysterious to us). It's also true that the major difference between Adam's applications to UNC, Oberlin, and lastly Grinnell and Macalester *were* the essays and the recordings of his compositions included in the latter applications.

I am very curious about the role the "essay" plays in admissions. Adam didn't want us to see his before he sent them off, but they were left on the computer afterward. Hence I'm attaching an essay he sent off to a couple of the latter schools which ended up being very enthusiastic about having Adam as a student.

In truth, the only quibble I'd have with the whole process at UNC is that someone might have asked why Adam's grades went down. In his case, he was thrown for an existential loop after Sept. 11. He couldn't understand why, at NCSSM where everyone, teachers and kids, seemed willing to discuss practically anything, hardly anyone wanted to talk about the implications and meaning of such a horrific event. He and a couple of friends tried to start an electronic magazine about student reactions but got no submissions other than their own. For Adam the combination of Sept. 11 and what he saw as a lack of response among his friends, peers, and teachers triggered what is called, we're told, a "reactive depression."

And yes, his grades suffered, because he felt that nothing mattered. And yes, it's also true that even before his depressive episode that Adam was not a "great" student. It's understandable that UNC wouldn't want to risk a scholarship. His study skills and organization still leave a lot to be desired. On the other hand we've also been told by more than one teacher that Adam has regularly demonstrated the intellectual curiosity, intuitive understanding, and the willingness to peer behind the "workings" of math to be a first rate mathematician.

In all honesty, we (the parents, with six UNC–CH degrees between us and generally pleased with what we got out of our various experiences there) think that Adam would probably do best going to a good small school for his first two years. He could then transfer into UNC for his junior and senior years. By then he'd be well prepared for upper and grad level courses that UNC's first rate math dept. has to offer. But the decision is his; and he does have a large number of friends going to UNC from S&M so we'll see.

To: Bob McConnaughey
From: Stephen Farmer

Thanks for your reply. I very much appreciate your account of Adam's reaction to the September 11 bombings, and I sympathize with the disappointment he experienced in comparing his classmates' reactions to his own and those of his close friends. In my experience—both personal and professional—I've never found high school to be a particularly welcoming forum for the fundamental questions impressed on us by tragedy. For what my opinion is worth, it's to Adam's great credit that he couldn't turn away from what he'd seen.

This essay is excellent. It highlights his curiosity and his thoughtfulness much more clearly than did his essays for us. The discrepancy is actually not that surprising to me, because I've seen it before in the applications of truly outstanding in-state students. Unfortunately, many of these students assume (rightly so, in most cases) that their admission to Carolina is something of a given, and they don't approach our essays as carefully as they might if we were, say, Harvard or Yale. As a result these students can be disadvantaged in the competition for honors selection, which does hinge, to a certain extent, on the curiosity, insight, and thoughtfulness we can glean from the essays.

As for whether Adam would be better served at a university or at a liberal-arts college, I think you're asking a good question—one I wish more parents and students asked. College admissions, in many quarters, now resembles trophy hunting more

> College admissions, in many quarters, now resembles trophy hunting more than good and careful matchmaking.

than good and careful matchmaking. I've long been an admirer of liberal-arts colleges and wish more students would explore them carefully.

Having said that, I'd also say that Carolina, despite its size, is better than all but a very few research universities in welcoming students and helping them get situated. I'd also add that, if Adam should decide to come to Carolina and want at least one adult contact as an initial resource, I'd be glad to help him in that way.

BENEFITS TO WEEKDAY VISITS

Because of various schedule conflicts, my daughter was not able to attend either Johns Hopkins' or Northwestern's Admitted Student events, so she scheduled visits on regular weekdays in April.

Hopkins assigned her a student to shadow for the day, who took her to classes, lunch with a group of ordinary students, and a visit to the dorm—not a showcase room, but one of the incredibly cramped rooms that most freshmen end up occupying.

While Northwestern didn't assign a student, she was able to sit in on classes and visit some of the student hangouts—as well as get a taste of Chicago's weather. By noon of that visit, she knew that the smaller campus and class environment at Hopkins was better for her, not to mention that it was a lot closer to home.

By *not* visiting during a structured event, we all felt that she got a more honest impression of both schools' academic and social life.

—JIM DELLON

April 29, 2002, 2:19 P.M.
To: Parents Forum at the North Carolina School of Science and
Mathematics
From: Bob McConnaughey

Well, Adam's mind was made up this late Fri. We flew out to
Minnesota and he visited Macalester. He sat in on an advanced
geometry class and really enjoyed it, talked to people in the
music department, and spent the night on campus. Adam liked
Grinnell a lot . . . but really *loved* Macalester.

    And so the decision was made—but not without some April
angst.

HEATHER'S ADVENTURE, PART 4

By May 1997, Heather Dresser had been wait-listed by Princeton and had decided against Washington University. That left the University of Virginia and Tufts.

    Virginia seemed the stronger of the two. She had been named a UVA Echols
scholar, meaning she could create her own major. As a Virginia resident, her tuition bill would be considerably lower, and she would have the comfort of knowing the hundreds of Jefferson High graduates already there or on their way. Tufts,
on the other hand, had been little more than an afterthought, the application
submitted because her parents said she needed more than four schools.

    But her weekend visit to Tufts's suburban Boston campus was a revelation. She
met dozens of students, many with her interest in international relations and foreign policy careers. An a *cappella* choral performance thrilled her. It was cold in
winter, but so what? And she did not like the idea of all of the familiar faces at
UVA. It would feel like grades 13 through 16 at Jefferson High.

(continues)

She sent in her acceptance form and check to Tufts and instantly got a dose of America's undying affection for brand-name schools.

"So where are you going, Heather?" a friend would ask.

"Tufts," she would say.

"Excuse me?"

"Tufts."

"Tufts? Where is Tufts? What is Tufts?"

"It's up near Boston. It has a great international relations program."

"Didn't you get into UVA?"

"Yeah."

"And you're not going there?"

"No."

Heather went to Boston a week early for a canoeing trip sponsored by the Tufts University Mountain Club. Orientation followed. The second week she tried out for the Jackson Jills, an all-female singing group with a rich history. Her audition was a success. Soon she forgot about Penn.

17

JAKE AND STEPHANIE TAKE A YEAR OFF

Delaying College

SOME HIGH SCHOOL seniors, having survived the college admission process, find themselves full of doubts by mid-May. They say to themselves, "What have I gotten myself into? Is college going to be just another academic grind? What am I going to do with my life?"

Most keep to their schedules and continue this conversation with themselves in college and beyond. But a few react differently. They get off the train. They delay college and try something else for a year.

This option has a long tradition. Moneyed households in nineteenth-century America often sent their sons, just graduated from boarding school, off for a year of travel in Europe before entering college or professional training. These days some of the most successful high school students delay matriculation for less expensive but nonetheless broadening experiences. They learn a musical

Few colleges object to students deferring enrollment for a year.

instrument, or work on a political campaign, or build houses, or pursue other nonacademic activities before beginning their lives as undergraduates.

Few colleges object to students deferring enrollment for a year. It means that the student is thinking seriously about her life and will arrive at college in a year even better prepared to add something significant to the college community.

JAKE'S JOURNEY

TWO RECENT HIGH school graduates I know took this route, for very different reasons. The first is Jake Jeppson, a slender and energetic alumnus of the Sidwell Friends School in Washington, D.C. He accepted an offer of admission from Middlebury but then became increasingly aware that he was not ready for the next step. "I'd become so wrapped up in the chase of the college admissions monster that I'd forgotten what college is all about—delving into materials and enriching myself by learning in an environment of my peers," he said. "I needed time away to regain perspective."

He found Cornelius Bull, head of the Cambridge, Massachusetts–based INTERIM programs. Uncertain teens like Jeppson were Bull's specialty. Bull had big bushy white sideburns and wore a safari suit. His office was filled with pictures of students smiling beside their sherpa guides on mountaintops, or swimming with dolphins, or meditating with monks. Behind him on the wall was a giant map of the world. Colored pins marked the places where he had sent students.

Jeppson spent two hours with Bull, but did not see anything he liked. On his own, he thought he had arranged a good internship with Habitat for Humanity, the house-building organization made famous by former president Jimmy Carter, in Jackson, West Virginia. But when Jeppson drove down there, he discovered that they wanted him to spend the year doing administrative work in an office rather than what he wanted to do, which was hammer nails. A plan to study World War I battlefields also fell through because of the chaos surrounding the events of September 11.

Eventually he found a job with the SEED (Schools for Educational Evolution and Development) Public Charter School in southeast Washington, D.C., handling paperwork in the development office and teaching a journalism class. It was an urban public boarding school with 154 students in grades 7 to 10. Jeppson made public relations packets. He produced an annual report. And he showed the yearbook staff (Sophia, Monique, Eboni-Rose, and Chantel) how to write and do desktop design.

His job at SEED forced him to spend long hours with his computer, often alone. He missed his friends. He exercised to dispel the blues. He became a runner. He found it was not so bad being on his own. When it came time to head for Vermont, he was ready. "The college admission process is a grueling one," he said. "Trying to find something to do with my year off was exhausting, and at times humiliating. Enduring a year without peers hurts. But, God, am I glad I did this."

STEPHANIE'S STORY

STEPHANIE MILLER, A red-haired graduate of the Potomac School in McLean, Virginia, chose to delay college for different reasons. She was heading for Trinity College in Hartford, Connecticut, but was not certain what she wished to study. In high school she had been a star of the drama department, with lead roles in *Kiss Me Kate* and *Guys and Dolls*. She had also been a member of the Madrigals singing group and of Quintessence, a five-woman *a cappella* group.

She thought she might want to act professionally, but she wasn't sure how to prepare for the stage while going to college. A year actually working in a theater, she thought, would be a good way to figure that out.

Larry Dow, the dean of admissions and financial aid at Trinity, said, "Although we don't automatically grant deferrals, we almost always find that the students' requests are thoughtful and even wise, and we almost always approve them as a result." He continued, "We've found that students who have the courage to question the 'one-timetable-fits-all' nature of the process are likely to be more explorative and purposeful when they do arrive at Trinity."

> Students who have the courage to question the "one-timetable-fits-all" nature of the process are likely to be more explorative and purposeful when they do arrive.

By June of Miller's high school senior year, she was already working as an intern at the Discovery Theater of the Smithsonian Institution, a small house that specializes in productions for children. She did everything: She took ticket orders, assisted patrons, and put out brochures. There was much to do backstage while she looked for auditions in local theaters to fill her evening hours.

Miller's father was not happy about her delaying college, at least not at first. "He thought I would lose motivation and never go to college at all," she said. But he changed his mind after he saw how hard she was working. Her mother, as well as many of her teachers, liked the idea. Her friends were amazed. "I wish I had the guts to do something like that," one said to her.

When her friends went off to Kenyon and Columbia and Sarah Lawrence and Rice in August, she felt the void. But they began to call her, and she realized she could stay in touch through the year, even if they were now on different schedules.

By then, she said, she realized she was learning much more than she could ever learn in a year of college about what life in the theater was really all about, and she would be ready to use all of Trinity's resources once she arrived the following year. She threw herself into several programs, but was particularly impressed by the Discovery Theater hosting of Deaf Way II, a week-long festival of deaf performers from all over the world.

It was art without words, a pure form of theater that Miller was happy she had not missed. "It was just amazing," she said. "I will be ready for anything now."

Obviously, delaying college for a year is not the right choice for every student. But entering college before you're ready may not be wise, either. Perhaps the best approach is to carefully consider what you want to learn—in life, in academics, and in your own growth as a human being—and then make the choice that is right for you.

> Carefully consider what you want to learn—in life, in academics, and in your own growth as a human being—and then make the choice that is right for you.

18

RETURNING YOUR COLLEGE TO THE STORE

Transferring

SARA BEDINGHAUS WAS looking for a good-sized university in an exciting city far from her home in Cincinnati. When Boston University and Tulane University both accepted her, she picked the well-regarded New Orleans school because it offered the bigger scholarship.

For many young Americans, Tulane would be a great choice. But it did not take Bedinghaus long to realize that for her, it was a mistake.

She had enjoyed the diversity of Walnut Hills High School, an academic magnet school that draws students from all over Cincinnati. By contrast, Tulane seemed full of white kids like her. The freshman courses were easier than what she had had at Walnut Hills. The women on campus had more money than she did and higher-priced tastes. "They wore expensive clothes, they had credit cards from their parents and $400 monthly allowances, which they didn't feel was enough to *survive*—honestly, someone said that. They all

> She did what sensible consumers do whenever a purchase does not please them. She took the product back. She transferred to another school.

joined sororities and had the means to go out to dinner or clubs every night," she said. And she heard white undergraduates make jokes that she did not like about black athletes.

"I had never been exposed to such ignorant, spoiled people as I met at Tulane," Bedinghaus said.

I doubt that the New Orleans university is anywhere near as shallow as Bedinghaus thinks it is. I suspect she just had bad luck in her dormitory room assignment. Nonetheless, she decided that Tulane was not for her, a personal decision that no one can question. And she did what sensible consumers do whenever a purchase does not please them. She took the product back. She transferred to another school.

FINDING THE RIGHT PLACE

I HAVE LONG wondered why the transfer option does not get more attention in college guides and articles about college admissions. U.S. Department of Education surveys indicate about a third of American undergraduates change colleges at least once. Many of those are community college students moving to four-year universities, but at least 20 percent of students like Bedinghaus who start in a four-year school transfer to another four-year school.

To me these are remarkably reassuring statistics. They provide one more reason why we parents, and our college-bound children, should not be working ourselves into such a frenzy over picking the right school. If it turns out to be a bad choice, all the student has to do is join the rather large group of young people who are switching to other colleges. Many college applicants make plans to transfer even before they enroll at their first school. They choose a relatively inexpensive state or community school for the first two years of basic courses, and then they move to more appropriate campuses for the specialized courses in their majors.

To repeat what I said in the introduction: Choosing a college is *not* like picking a spouse. Making the wrong choice does not condemn you to a life of sorrow or an emotionally and financially wrenching divorce. Choosing a college is, rather, like buying a house. If you decide that you need more bathrooms or the neighbors are just intolerable, it is a relatively simple matter to sell the place and buy another one.

That is what Bedinghaus did. She switched to the University of Cincinnati. She decided she preferred her diverse group of old friends and the lower-priced values of the urban Midwest to what she encountered in the Big Easy.

> About a third of American undergraduates change colleges at least once.

KNOWING WHEN—AND WHERE— TO TRANSFER

A FINE BOOK to fill the void of information about changing schools is *How to Transfer to the College of Your Choice* by Eric Freedman (Ten Speed Press, 2002). Freedman, a journalism professor at Michigan State, analyzes each stage in the process and describes the different transfer policies at different schools.

Most universities welcome transfers. They fill dorm rooms and lecture hall seats left empty by first- or second-year students who drop out or transfer themselves. Transfers are older, more experienced, and more likely to appreciate what their new school has to offer. Some state universities are rated on how many transfers they receive, because community colleges will not prosper if state universities are not welcoming their graduates.

BENEFITS OF TRANSFERRING

I started out as a freshman at UCLA, but I had grown up in Oregon and was not ready to live in Los Angeles. I felt obligated to stay there because I felt lucky to have been accepted as an out-of-state student and my mom had gone there. Luckily, my parents were smart enough to realize that I was not happy there and that transferring schools could easily be done. So I switched between terms and started at the University of Oregon for the last trimester of my freshman year.

Benefits? Tons cheaper, all my AP high school credits transferred over (whereas UCLA would not accept them), and the Ducks eventually started beating the Bruins in football. So it was a wise choice. All in all, the transfer was very easy to accomplish. The funny thing is that when applying to colleges in the first place, I never considered an in-state school, which I think is a mistake that lots of successful high school students make.

—AMITY CLAUSEN

But each campus is different. Here is a chart showing how many transfers were accepted by some well-known schools in 2000, as well as the percentage of total transfer applications that number represented, and how that percentage compared to the percentage of freshman applicants accepted. I start with the more welcoming colleges and work my way down.

The chart shows there is no point in trying to switch to Princeton. An unexpected jump in freshmen accepting admission offers has left that university with no room for transfers in recent years. And some selective schools are choosier in admitting transfers than they are in picking freshmen.

School	Transfers Accepted	Percentage Accepted	Percentage Freshman Applicants Accepted
Notre Dame	210	53	34
Davidson	17	50	36
Cornell	754	38	31
Georgetown	424	32	22
Northwestern	166	31	33
Brown	200	29	16
Wesleyan	118	28	27
Wellesley	27	26	43
Pennsylvania	380	24	23
Dartmouth	55	23	21
Washington & Lee	13	20	35
Rice	78	15	23
Swarthmore	17	15	24
Caltech	22	15	13
MIT	43	15	19
Johns Hopkins	54	14	32
Williams	10	13	24
Bates	17	12	29
Middlebury	27	10	23
Stanford	113	9	13
Duke	23	8	26
Columbia	63	7	13
Cooper Union	46	7	13
Harvard	73	6	11
Amherst	10	5	19
Yale	36	5	16
Haverford	3	4	32
Princeton	0	0	12

Sources: *America's Elite Colleges* and *The Best 331 Colleges* (Random House, 2001)

DIFFERENT FOLKS, DIFFERENT STROKES

I started at Princeton University in the fall of 1993. I was deciding between there and some other, smaller colleges, but I picked Princeton because I thought I might want to do the engineering program, which most small colleges don't offer. . . . When I arrived, I found that it wasn't what I expected. The social dynamics of the place weren't what I wanted and the amount of "face time" you got with professors, at least as a freshman, was minimal. I also wanted to play a varsity sport [lacrosse] and was surprised (admittedly, this was my own fault for not checking) at how time-consuming and competitive this was in the academically minded Ivy League. I also decided I didn't want to be an engineer.

Anyway, I went to visit my friend at Williams College during my fall break and really liked it there. . . . I had visited Williams during my college touring during high school and fell in love with it, but was worried it was too small. I transferred there for my sophomore through senior years and had a wonderful experience academically, socially, and athletically. This isn't to knock Princeton—it's a great school—but it wasn't right for me.

—HILARY BROWNE-HUTCHINSON

LOOKING FOR GROWTH

SOME VERY SELECTIVE schools still actively encourage transfers, however. The vast majority of American four-year colleges have opened their doors to people who want to switch, evidenced by the fact that one out of every five members of their student bodies started somewhere else.

Selective schools are unlikely to take an applicant as a transfer if they rejected that person before *unless*—and this exception should not be overlooked—the person has grown in some significant way. I am not just talking about a community college basketball star who is now a foot taller than he was in twelfth grade. Strong first-year college grades can erase the stain of a mediocre high school transcript. New attitudes, new interests, and new accomplishments impress admissions officers. They look for transfer applicants with a serious academic interest not well served by their current college.

Robert L. Cummings, of Dunbar Educational Consultants in New Canaan, Connecticut, said, "We have worked with quite a few college students who successfully transferred after their freshman year, in many cases to considerably more selective colleges than their first college. In all cases, they achieved very strong grades—generally A's in non-fluff courses—during their first semester as a freshman.

> Selective schools are unlikely to take an applicant as a transfer if they rejected that person before *unless*—and this exception should not be overlooked—the person has grown in some significant way.

"Our feeling is that even the most selective colleges value success at the college level and are therefore more apt to accept transfer applicants who have proven they can do excellent college work even at 'lesser' colleges," he continued. "In several cases, students were accepted as transfers by colleges that had denied them the previous year, but they all got A's in their freshman year."

Admittedly, transferring after just one year requires quick thinking. Many find it more comfortable to switch after the sophomore year. Making certain the new school gives you credit for your courses at the old school is also important, but Freedman says universities are easing their credit transfer rules. If you are thinking of transferring, he says, you ought to call the school you have in mind right away and ask its experts which of your credits they will accept.

YOU'RE NOT STUCK

THE IMPORTANT THING is remembering you are not stuck with your original choice. Flummoxed parents should keep that in mind when their recently departed offspring calls from school in October and says he is miserable. The usual response from unimaginative dads like me is, "Well, it can't be that bad," or "Maybe you just need to give it more time," or "We can talk about it when you come home for Thanksgiving." But if you say, "Well, maybe you should look into transferring to another school," the anguished child is reminded that there is something he can do about the problem. If he does the research, he may change schools or he may discover that what he wants requires another course of action. At least he is nudged into doing something more positive than just making you miserable.

Some parents may be saying, "Isn't that just giving up? Why not tell him to suck it up and tough it out?" Let's see. Conduct this thought experiment. You have placed your order at an expensive restaurant. The steak you are served is severely overcooked. Do you just tell yourself to chew harder?

> Picking a particular college is in some ways little more than a very pricey shopping trip. Don't make more of it than is necessary.

Going to college is an important life choice. But picking a particular college is in some ways little more than a very pricey shopping trip. Don't make more of it than is necessary.

Julie Aldrich, who lives in Meriden, Connecticut, remembers her daughter Katherine calling in great distress after the student's first week at Hamilton College, a small, well-regarded, upstate New York college. Aldrich wrote this off as the usual first-week jitters, similar to what Katherine had experienced when she went off to boarding school in the ninth grade.

Fortunately for Aldrich, Katherine was very self-reliant. In October she called to say that she had ordered some college guide books "so that I wouldn't be shocked when I got the credit card bill and, oh, by the way, it was snowing," Aldrich recalled.

"She was convinced that she wanted to transfer," Aldrich said. "I said all the right things about waiting a while, giving the school a chance, and on and on. She came back with reasoned arguments about why this was the wrong school for her. On the one hand, she felt it would be easier to stay where she was than to do the application process all over again and that if she stayed, she would succeed there. But she would feel she was settling, and she did not want to live with regret. I couldn't argue with that logic."

A LEARNING EXPERIENCE, NOT A MISTAKE

IN JANUARY, KATHERINE called to ask her mother what she thought of George Washington University in Washington, D.C. And she added, "It's still snowing, Mom." She wanted to major in political science. Washington was where the action was. She arranged a visit and found that she loved the city, loved the school, loved the proximity of good shopping in Georgetown, and loved the relative infrequency of white frozen water crystals falling from the sky. She applied and was accepted. Aldrich and her husband had not seen the campus, but they realized their daughter knew what she was doing and wrote the check.

When the family arrived at GW last summer, "A well-organized transfer orientation provided much needed information, the administration and staff made us feel very much at ease leaving her in a strange city, and we left excited for her and for the opportunities the city and the university could offer," Aldrich said. "She looks at her first year of college as a learning experience rather than a mistake and recognizes that it was an opportunity for her to more clearly define her needs and desires. . . . She has become much more focused and goal oriented. It was the best move she could have made."

In this era of venture capital and technological shifts and down-sizing, students like Katherine have to be ready for changes in their jobs and locations. They are not too young to be getting some experience in making the smart move. That seems to me much better than staying where they are and calling their parents every week to say how much they hate their lives.

TWO VIEWS OF ONE SCHOOL

The following two transfer accounts, involving the same college, demonstrate eloquently that it's the student, not the school, that matters:

My life has been one constant move. Born in Spain, I grew up in California, North Carolina, Italy, Michigan, and Virginia, and my family finally settled down in Inwood, West Virginia. I graduated from high school 33rd out of a class of 212 and went on to my number one and only choice, St. Mary's College [SMC] of Maryland. It was the only school I ever wanted to attend. It seemed to incorporate every ideal I had. It was small, diverse, committed to excellence, and, supposedly, one of the best colleges in the country.

I went into my freshman year with high hopes, which were then dashed within weeks. Only on paper did this school embrace diversity. In actuality, the school was three-quarters white, upper-class, metro-area suburbanites. They were used to relying on their parents for everything, from food to booze to their education. I, however, was footing the whole bill, all $21,000 of it—in loans. As my freshman year ended, I went back to West Virginia with every intention of returning to SMC.

A month into summer break, I startled my family with the announcement that I was not going back to St. Mary's. Instead, I was going back to my roots and had applied to West Virginia University. . . . As I left for Morgantown, West Virginia, in the fall, I was thinking, "What the hell am I doing? I made some great friends at SMC and now, all of a sudden, I'm a freshman again." Thankfully, credit-wise, I made out because St. Mary's had four-credit classes, so I was a super-sophomore. WVU is 22,000 strong, in comparison to SMC's 1,600. They have all races, religions, and have demographics from all fifty states and the District of Columbia, as well as forty-five-plus other countries. They have a group for everyone.

Would I make the same decision again? Though I learned a lot about my wants and needs by going to SMC, the only thing I would have done differently is to never have gone.

—ALYSSA D. RICE

Both my sister and I transferred colleges. I had a difficult situation in which my first-choice college did not provide any financial aid (Boston University), so I decided to go to my hometown college (Virginia Commonwealth University [VCU]). After two years there, I was suffocating and felt that I wasn't being challenged enough by the schoolwork, so I decided to transfer. I chose St. Mary's College of Maryland. That school quite literally saved my life. It was a much more challenging and supportive atmosphere, not to mention a beautiful campus. The admissions department made it easy to transfer (easier than applying as a freshman!) and those were the best two years of my life so far.

Transferring is also a good way to get a more well-rounded college experience. I went from a huge commuter school with almost no on-campus activities to a small liberal arts honors college with a strong community ethic. I found that the lack of diversity in class offerings was more than offset by the quality of the students, teachers, and staff at SMC. While at VCU, due to the rigors of the music program, I was able to determine that the life of a professional musician wasn't for me. I probably wouldn't have discovered this at SMC, where the program is much smaller and less well-known. I am much happier with my music being a part of who I am, rather than what I do.

—SARAH NESNOW

19

MAKE YOUR
OWN HARVARD

GREG FORBES SIEGMAN was doing fine until the spring of his senior year in 1990. He was near the top of his class at a very competitive public high school in the Chicago suburbs. His list of activities was impressive. It appeared he would go to a great college and do important work.

His dreams were those of many high school academic stars in the college-conscious United States. He would go to one of the Ivy League schools, or maybe Stanford. He would go to law school, or maybe film school. He would argue a case before the U.S. Supreme Court, or maybe win an Academy Award. The presidency was not impossible.

But then the letters began arriving from the very selective colleges he had applied to. Each was distressingly thin. Each was a rejection. He could not believe it. Had there been a mistake? The gut-churning truth, when it reached him soon after, was even worse than not knowing.

One of the teachers he had asked to write recommendations told Siegman he had decided, on his own, that no matter how much the teenager believed in his dreams, the teacher thought they were out of whack. The teacher had told the colleges that Siegman was a nice enough young man and worked very hard for his grades, but he did not have the intellectual capacity to flourish at such schools. He was not Ivy League material.

"NOT IVY LEAGUE MATERIAL . . ."

THERE ARE MANY Greg Forbes Siegmans. America is a country built on supersized ambition. The 120-pound water boy thinks he can be quarterback. The book store clerk dreams of writing the great American novel. The high school dropout is certain he will win a Grammy and live in Bel Air.

The college admissions process is designed to bring all those hopes in line with reality. Siegman's teacher probably thought he was doing Siegman a favor. If he went to Harvard, the teacher figured, he would only be disappointed and struggle against his limits without any hope of reward.

The huge tub of bile that fell on Siegman senior year has had an extraordinary effect on him. But on November 10, 2002, he passed a milestone. When Siegman was twenty-four, working as a part-time restaurant doorman and just starting as a substitute teacher in one of the poorest neighborhoods in Chicago, he decided to start a mentoring program called brunchbunch.com. He invited people of different backgrounds to weekly meals designed to break down stereotypes and other psychological and social barricades. After seventy weeks of successful brunches, in which young professionals forged deep relationships with young people needing mentors, Siegman set up a foundation. It supervises the brunchbunch.com program and raises money so young people can get the opportunity he was denied to attend their first-choice colleges.

He called it the 11-10-02 Foundation, celebrating the day that he would turn thirty and his belief that people under thirty were as capable as anyone to do anything. By that date he was resolved to have made a difference in the world, no matter what his high school teacher had thought, no matter how unrealistic his dreams still seemed to many of the people he met.

Naturally, long before the deadline, his optimism and energy had exactly the desired effect. Not only did the weekly brunches change many lives, but the foundation raised more than $250,000 to further the cause. His ShakingUpChicago.com Scholarship Program gave out tens of thousands of dollars in college grants.

In 1999, Siegman was honored by Hasbro as a real-life American hero. In 2000, he became the youngest adult in the country to be honored at the National Jefferson Awards for Public Service. He was named a Man of Distinction by Zeta Beta Tau in 2001. In 2002, he was honored as one of America's Points of Light.

Also in 2002, he finally got the degree he had been looking for. As a deeply disappointed high school graduate, he had talked his way into Tulane University in New Orleans, and started his community work there. He won election to the student senate and joined a fraternity. But after two years he left Tulane. He was still consumed with the desire to prove he belonged at an Ivy League–type school.

IVY ENVY

SIEGMAN SHOWED UP unannounced on the campus of Northwestern University, a very selective school north of Chicago, and proceeded to talk his way into a place at that school, too. His undergraduate record was spectacular—thirty-seven A's and a B-plus. One would have thought he would be overjoyed by his success. Instead, he was miserable and refused to attend his graduation at Northwestern, the sort of big name university he had always craved.

He realized, to his astonishment, what the reason was. He missed Tulane. He had loved the vibrancy of New Orleans, the student politics, and the many opportunities for community service. It finally occurred to him, after many years of Ivy envy, that the brand-name value of a school had nothing to do with what made it memorable.

> It finally occurred to him, after many years of Ivy envy, that the brand-name value of a school had nothing to do with what made it memorable.

So six years later when Prairie State College in Chicago Heights invited him to be its graduation speaker, the youngest in its history, he took this to be his second chance to cross a stage at graduation—and one he was not going to pass up. Ivy League degree or not, he had arrived. At the age of twenty-nine, he was getting an honorary degree. He told his story and received a standing ovation. Paul J. McCarthy, the president of Prairie State, said Siegman's story was "a testament to what one person can accomplish if they are willing to put in the time it takes to reach their goal."

Which is exactly what any disappointed high school senior should keep in mind as he stares glumly at the thin envelope that holds the rejection letter from his first-choice college. It does not matter where you go to school. It matters what you do when you get there, and what you do after you graduate, and what you do with the gift of time, millions of dollars' worth of time, that most of us are given.

THE "SPIELBERG EFFECT"

THERE IS NOW a term for this phenomenon, invented by Stacy Berg Dale and Alan Krueger, the researchers who discovered that students who were accepted at selective colleges but attended other schools did just as well financially after twenty years as those who went to those well-known colleges.

In 1965, a scrawny, bespectacled senior at Saratoga High School near San Jose, California, applied to the famous film school at UCLA. He thought he was good enough, but his grades were mediocre and the school rejected him. He went to Long Beach State (later to become California State University–Long Beach) instead, still thinking about a way to create the career he had in mind. He later tried to transfer from Long Beach State to another famous film school, the University of Southern California, but again he was rejected.

> It does not matter where you go to school. It matters what you do when you get there, and what you do after you graduate, and what you do with the gift of time, millions of dollars' worth of time, that most of us are given.

While looking at their data, Dale and Krueger noticed something odd about students like him. In many cases, they found that even applicants who were rejected by brand-name schools did as well in later life as those who were accepted.

The researchers began to wonder whether students' sense of themselves made admissions committees' opinions less important. Under this theory, if you applied to Columbia, Wellesley, and Swarthmore, then you were by definition Columbia, Wellesley, and Swarthmore material, even if those schools spurned you and you had to make do with Cleveland State.

The notion deserved further study, they decided. In the meantime, they gave it a label. It seemed fitting to use the name of the Long Beach State student who was disappointed by his college rejections but managed to do something with his time anyway. He made five films at Long Beach State, crashed some of the student film screenings at USC, and pushed the studio executives so hard that eventually he got a chance to show what he could do when allowed to make a real feature film.

His name was Steven Spielberg. Dale and Krueger dubbed the phenomenon of rejected college applicants succeeding in spite of their disappointment the "Spielberg effect." Just like Siegman, Spielberg eventually got to star at a graduation ceremony. In 2002 he put on a cap and gown, and, with music from *Indiana Jones* blaring over loudspeakers at the Cal State Long Beach ceremonies, Spielberg received a bachelor's degree in film and electronic arts, the final requirements completed through independent studies turned in under a pseudonym.

> Their successes had almost nothing to do with where they did, or did not, go to college.

That degree, of course, meant little when compared to Spielberg's body of work. The same goes for Siegman's degree from Prairie State, although Siegman admitted it made him feel good to know that Spielberg, one of his heroes, had followed a similar path. Filmmaking was one of Siegman's many interests. He screened a movie about his community activities on his all-important thirtieth birthday in 2002.

Spielberg and Siegman were what they did. Their legacies are the people they have helped and the lessons and images they have brought to life. And it should be obvious by now, to anyone who is paying attention, that their successes had almost nothing to do with where they did, or did not, go to college.

WHAT DOES IT ALL MEAN?

SO, AFTER THIS winding journey through the college admissions process, where do we find ourselves? It appears that deeply entrenched perceptions are not easy to change. Shortly before I finished this book, *Worth* magazine published a remarkable article entitled "Getting Inside the Ivy Gates." It was well-written and brilliantly researched, and it proved, just by the way the magazine promoted the article, that my efforts to dampen the American lust for brand-name colleges have been an embarrassing flop.

The line on the top of the magazine's cover said "Special Report: How to Get Your Kid into Harvard." On the table of contents page was a gorgeous photograph of a stately Ivy League building looming over a summery lawn, with this quote: "Private schools have a far better record than public schools do of placing kids at Harvard, Yale, and Princeton." The first page of the article promised to reveal "what all parents need to know about getting their children into America's most elite colleges."

Then *Worth* presented its analysis and a list of the one hundred top high schools in America, as measured by their success in sending their graduates to Harvard, Yale, and Princeton.

WHAT'S HOT AND WHAT'S NOT

I THINK THE article was about fashion—our consumer sense of what's hot and what's not—and not about education. I am not saying you cannot learn something at Harvard. I spent three years there as an undergraduate and two more at its graduate school. I earn a living as a reporter because of the journalism practice I had at Harvard's student newspaper. But you can find many books on the shelf that are better written and researched than this one, and the vast majority of their authors did not go to Harvard or any other Ivy League school.

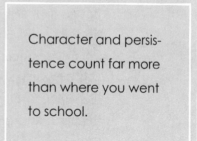

Character and persistence count far more than where you went to school.

This is a country, thank goodness, where character and persistence count far more than where you went to school. What confuses the issue is that the big-name schools look for character and persistence in their admissions process and then accept much credit (while making a great show of not doing so) when the forthright and indefatigable young people they admit to their schools turn out to be big successes.

The private high schools that send so many of their graduates to the Ivies play the same game. *Worth* magazine editor-in-chief John Koten and *Worth* writer Reshma Memon Yaqub found an ingenious way to count how many Harvard-Yale-Princeton students came from which high school. They got their hands on the face books—the official guides to the freshman classes—and noted the high school listed under each name and photograph. The top one hundred pipeline-to-the-big-three-Ivies high schools included only six public schools. Two of those, Hunter College High in New York City and Jefferson in northern Virginia, admit only the highest-scoring applicants, and the other four draw from the affluent enclaves of Princeton, New Jersey; Scarsdale, New York; Bronxville, New York; and Millburn, New Jersey.

The article said this proves that very expensive private schools (many on the list charged about $20,000 a year) have an inside track to the Ivies. Their counselors are more likely to know the college admissions officers, and those admissions staffers are more likely to visit them than other high schools. Their students are more likely to have the most help preparing for the SAT and writing their essays.

Such advantages are real, but anyone who thinks about this for a while or has read this book can see that those perks have little to do with getting into Harvard, Yale, and Princeton. Those three schools, for all their self-regard, are not the favorite colleges of the majority of the nation's best high school seniors. That is why the three schools spend so much money (as we saw in chapter 5) on letters to juniors with high SAT and ACT scores, urging them to apply. Stanford, Brown, Columbia, Amherst, and several other schools, including no-names like little Cooper Union, a tuition-free school in Manhattan, are just as competitive in admissions as the Big Three. Harvard, Yale, and Princeton are among the most successful in persuading students to accept their offers of admission, but a fifth of Harvard admittees and a third of Yale and Princeton admitees still go somewhere else.

And here is the key point, the central argument of this book: Those private schools do well in getting kids into the most selective colleges because they already have much more than their share of the kind of students those colleges want. Parents send their children to private high schools like Dalton or Exeter or St. Albans in part *because* they want them to go to colleges like Harvard, Yale, and Princeton. That means those high schools will have more students focused on that goal. They don't want to go to another school that is just as good, like Berkeley or Michigan or Maryland. They want to go to Harvard, Yale, or Princeton, and no other.

> Those private schools do well in getting kids into the most selective colleges because they already have much more than their share of the kind of students those colleges want.

As I have said, the private high schools have already creamed off great dollops of teenagers whose grades, test scores, and other talents are most likely to please the Big Ivies. Those young people are more likely to have parents who went to one of those schools, another advantage they have in this very narrow-minded contest.

This fierce grab for the well-known name, we know from the research, leads nowhere that the student would not have reached on his or her own merits. The *Worth* magazine suggestion of elitist advantage, and the overall American belief in the power of the Ivies, is severely misplaced.

WHO REALLY HAS THE INSIDE TRACK?

KEEP THIS ASTONISHING fact in mind. Better yet, make a copy of this paragraph and keep it in your wallet. Whatever the hoopla over Ivy magic and private school influence, students who remain in public high schools, particularly the less competitive ones, still have an advantage over students with similar records at the private schools on the *Worth* list when it comes to applying to selective colleges.

Remember, the largest study of this phenomenon, Paul Attewell's analysis of 1,196,213 members of the high school graduating class of

1997, found that a student at a public school you never heard of was more likely to get into a selective college than a student at Groton or Sidwell Friends or Harvard-Westlake with the same SAT scores. The reason was that the public school senior would have a much higher class rank and stand out in a way that the private school student, competing with dozens of classmates, would not.

> Whatever the hoopla over Ivy magic and private school influence, students who remain in public high schools, particularly the less competitive ones, still have an advantage over students with similar records at the private schools on the *Worth* list when it comes to applying to selective colleges.

The Dale-Krueger and Attewell studies I explored in chapters 1 and 2, as well as all the other evidence in these pages, show that the rich kids with high SAT scores do not inherit the Earth. Power instead goes to hardworking students from all kinds of families who aren't discouraged by bad breaks.

Most people reading this, at whatever age, have already figured that out. Those of us who have been in the workforce for some time can see that our bosses are far more likely to have attended a tax-supported institution than some ancient school with a fat endowment. Even teenagers know that the kids who do well are those who do their homework and come to practice.

I think, and there is some tentative research to back me up, that we revere Harvard, Yale, Princeton, and colleges like them because we are tribal animals who need a pecking order. But social evolution has given us the power to joke about it, and hopefully we are nearly at the point where prestige, whatever that is, will no longer have such weight when we apply to colleges.

WHAT REALLY MATTERS IN CHOOSING YOUR COLLEGE

I ATTENDED A little-known college and then a well-known college. I have spent much time inside huge, underfunded state schools and also inside private schools with wood-paneled offices. I am convinced that the best college to attend is the one that looks like an adventure, a place that will take you where you have always wanted to go. The worst college to attend is the one your friends say you cannot turn down.

Look closely at Harvard, or any other school with a similar reputation, and you will find it is not *what* it is teaching but *whom* it is teaching that makes it look so good. Wherever you decide is best for you, there will be many others with similar ambitions and similar drives. Knowing you have something to give the world is all that you need to have a great college experience.

> The best college to attend is the one that looks like an adventure, a place that will take you where you have always wanted to go. The worst college to attend is the one your friends say you cannot turn down.

Learn what you want to do in life and how. Hundreds of great schools are ready to help you. Your actions will give a luster to whatever college you have chosen, and perhaps someday that school will be the one everyone is talking about, without anyone noticing that it was people like you who made it that way.

HEATHER'S ADVENTURE, PART 5

Heather Dresser received her bachelor's degree *summa cum laude* from Tufts in international relations and quantitative economics on a warm spring day in 2001 with her parents and brother happily applauding. She moved right into a great job, as a research assistant with the American Enterprise Institute, one of Washington's leading think tanks.

Her time at Tufts was a triumph. She kept her Japanese studies going. The international relations courses were superb. And her musical group, the Jackson Jills, was even better.

(continues)

Two of their albums won Contemporary *A Cappella* Recording Awards. The repertoire was pop contemporary, including Bon Jovi's "You Give Love a Bad Name," Gladys Knight and the Pips's "Midnight Train to Georgia," Tori Amos's "Crucify," and Dresser's sultry solo on the Nina Gordon hit "Tonight and the Rest of My Life." When the Jills were in high gear, their black dresses shining, their harmonies blending, the audience's feet tapping, Heather couldn't imagine being anywhere else.

She thought her success in getting the postgraduation job she wanted was the result of her summer internships. Her Japanese skills won her a summer spot with Mitsui in Washington after her freshman year. She worked for an economic consulting firm after her sophomore year. Following her junior year, she worked for an importer and distributor of electronic components in Boston owned by a Tufts alumnus.

Back at Jefferson, her old high school, where Tufts was still thought of as a lesser school, the anxiety level of high school seniors was worse than ever. Applications to Penn, the first-choice school Heather did not get into, were up 65 percent in the four years since she had applied, and the demand for some of the other Ivies was even higher.

If she were asked to address an assembly of anxious parents and students, Heather said, she would speak of the sanity and self-confidence that come with picking a school for what it has to offer, rather than how it will look on a resume.

"It's the person," she said. "It doesn't matter where they go to college."

APPENDIX A

*Twenty Not-So-Easy Questions
to Guide Your Search*

IN ANY INVESTIGATION, it is hard to tell what questions you should have asked first until you are almost done asking. Having been through the college admissions process a few times as a parent and interviewer and having talked to scores of experts, let me suggest 20 things you should ask yourself—10 questions for students and 10 questions for parents.

You will notice that I do not provide different scores for different answers, as do many of those magazines we buy at the supermarket. I do not even suggest in many cases what are the right answers. That is up to you. But I think these intimate inquiries—things to ask yourself, or your family members—will help you decide what to do.

TEN QUESTIONS FOR STUDENTS

1. Am I ready for college?

No quick answers, please. You have to think about this. It is something you should ask yourself when your friends, and maybe your parents, are pushing you to pick a college to which you can apply early decision. You may be unable to decide on which school is your first choice, but there is more to it than that. The whole idea of college may be vague to you. You may be too caught up in the more immediate moments of your life, a big date on Friday, a big game on Saturday, a big test on Monday. So wait before you answer. (It is okay to apply before you have an answer. Applying does not restrict your options.) And if you find it is December or January and you still are not sure, keeping thinking and talking to people, and asking yourself the questions below.

2. Do I have the faintest idea what I want to do with my life?

This is a fun question, actually. If the answer is no, you need not worry. One of the things colleges do best is help you sort out where you want to go after college. But if you think you know what kind of life you want to lead, hold that in your mind whenever you check out schools you might want to attend. This seems so obvious as to be almost insulting, but many students get caught up in a campus' look or reputation and don't think very carefully about how it fits them. I wanted to go to China when I was 18, and yet did not apply to a school that offered Chinese. I am still not sure why.

3. Do I like exploring strange places, or do I prefer getting to know the people near me very well?

This is my way of asking the old "big school or small school" question. I am biased in favor of big schools, or consortiums of small schools, that allow a student to explore many fields and activities and switch from one to another as they learn more about what they want. But you need a school that feels right, and if you are the sort of person who likes strong attachments to a few people and a few activities, and who dislikes noise and distraction, a bigger school might not be the best thing, at least for now. Think about who you are and act accordingly.

4. Do I care how far I will be from my family?

I think it is a very important consideration for many students and should be addressed frankly. If you don't want to be too far away, say so. Ties to community are extremely important. They are often the basis of happy lives and should not be cast aside just because your best friend is going to a school 2,000 miles away and calling you a homebody.

5. Do I live in a city, a suburb or the country, and do I like it there?

Usually your parents or counselors will ask if you want to go to school in a city, a suburb, or the country. I think the better question is: How do you like the place in which you live and study now? College is a good time to try something different, but if you are happy with where you are, you might have at least one school on your list that is in the same sort of place.

6. Do I want to be with a lot of students who are like me, or not?

This seems almost like question 4, but it's not. Many colleges promise diverse student bodies, but diversity for you may not be diversity for me. My first college was in California, full of other Californians, and not too different for me. But my roommate from Chicago thought it was a very exotic place. This is a version of the familiar question, do you want to be close to home or not? American culture has made the main roads of Fairfax, Va., Naperville, Ill., and Anaheim, Calif., look alike, but the habits and assumptions of people in different parts of the country still vary, and you have to think about what you want.

7. Am I willing to consider transferring to another college if my first one doesn't work?

I think it is important, in your thinking about college, to consider the possibility that you may eventually attend more than one school. If for some reason the notion of transferring does not appeal to you, then you are going to have to be extraordinarily careful in your selection. I think the wise answer to the question above is yes because you cannot anticipate everything that will happen to you.

8. Am I worried about my family being able to afford college?

This is a concern many students have. They ought to be frank about it with themselves and their parents. There are many ways to handle the financial demands of college. Parents should know about their children's concerns about money and give them as realistic a picture as possible. By the same token students should not be making decisions about which school they will attend based on mistaken assumptions that their family cannot afford schools that appeal to them.

9. Does it matter to me if a college has a famous name?

The main message of this book is that the name should not matter. But denying one's deepest feelings is always a bad idea. If you need brand names, admit it, and pick your colleges accordingly. Just stay away from me when you do so because I will try to change your mind.

10. Will I be troubled by a campus where drinking and sex are common?

I was not bothered by the recreational activities of my fellow undergraduates when I was in college, as long as they did not wake me or mess up the hallway. But both binge drinking and unsafe sex have drawn more attention in recent years and some schools have made concerted efforts to reduce the chances of harm. Very few schools have been successful in this regard, but a few that have are among those listed at the back of this book. Although some guidebooks seem to celebrate those schools with reputations for celebratory weekends, many people look back fondly on their college years for reasons that have nothing to do with how many times they embarrassed themselves.

TEN QUESTIONS FOR PARENTS

1. Are we ready for our child to go to college?

A lot of us say we are, but aren't. The process will go more smoothly if we recognize how unhappy we are about our children making preparations to leave us. We should keep that in mind when we are about to start a big fight with our child about the proper typing fonts for her essay or the importance of visiting Aunt Ida's alma mater.

2. **During the last two years of high school, are we worrying more about our child's grades and test scores or about how much he or she is being challenged in high school courses?**

The amount of challenge in a course is more important that the grade our child gets. As long as he or she is doing the work, getting a lower grade than we had hoped for is a minor annoyance. Our child will be a better student for having worked hard at a difficult subject. Colleges will appreciate that, and the best study of college completions rates shows that those students most likely to get their bachelor's degrees are not those with the best high school grades or test scores, but the ones who took the most difficult courses.

3. **Are we willing to support our child's college decision?**

We can help with the research on different college programs. We can offer advice. We can go on the college tours and listen to the information sessions. But other than setting the financial limits, we can't pick the school. If we try to do so, we risk estrangement and, even worse, the possibility that our child will lose valuable time and emotional security by going to a place that is not right for him. The best approach is to support whatever he decides, within reason, and let him transfer if it turns out to be a mistake.

4. **Are we willing to let our child take the lead in the college search, including which schools to visit, which to apply to, and how to fill out the application?**

Parents can play a role. But we are asking for trouble if we try to take charge of the process. In some cases, if the student is dragging her feet, leadership is necessary, but it might be more useful—if we are up to it—to let her miss some deadlines and suffer the consequences. She may not be ready for college, and this is one way to tell. Okay, this is not a suggestion even I would take, but it is an interesting thought.

5. Are we willing to make financial sacrifices so that our child can attend whichever school she wants?

You have to think through the money question and be very sure that your child knows what you are thinking. Often students get the wrong idea about their parents' finances and make bad decisions because of their ignorance.

6. Do we feel strongly that our child should attend a state school?

Again, discuss this with the applicant. But also listen to what he says.

7. Do we feel strongly that our child should not go too far from home, and what is too far?

This again is an important consideration. We parents should be clear about what we think and make this clear to our child. But I think we should send our children to any good colleges they choose that we can afford.

8. Will we be unhappy if our child does not at least apply to our college?

An easy compromise for those parents who yearn to send offspring to their alma mater is to promise not to make them go if they will at least agree to apply.

9. Will we be troubled by a campus where drinking and sex are common?

This is a good discussion to have with our children, if for no other reason than to prepare them for what is, in many minds, the

worst aspect of an otherwise fine system of higher education—
unhealthy social behavior, often reinforced by youth culture and
rarely drawing university sanctions.

**10. Can we stand it if, at the last moment, our child picks the
school at the bottom of our list?**

Responsible parents who involve themselves in the admissions
process often form opinions at the end of it. Sometimes our views
are not the same as the applicant's. It is best to begin preparing ourselves, right from the start, for eventual disappointment, so we do
not behave too badly when it comes.

APPENDIX B: HIDDEN GEMS

100 Colleges That Are Better Than You Think

*I*HAVE SPENT much of this book deriding the notion that successful marketing equals academic excellence and reminding readers that they should choose colleges based not on fame, but whether the schools fulfill their personal desires and dreams. We all know the big brand names. Once you have decided they are not right for you, where then should you be applying?

The list below is an attempt to answer that excellent question. In my *Washington Post* online column "Class Struggle" [washington post.com/wp-dyn/education/columns/classstruggles/], I asked guidance counselors and teachers who work with college-bound students to tell me which schools deserved bigger reputations. I was looking for what Shirley Bloomquist and Sunny Greene, former guidance officials at the Thomas Jefferson High School for Science and Technology in Fairfax County, Va., called the "lesser-known jewels." Bloomquist and Greene spent a great deal of time and energy introducing students to the wallflower colleges that many students fall in love with once they get to know them. I asked counselors and teachers to tell me what their graduates, dropping by for a visit, had told them about under-appreciated schools. Each was asked to name as many as ten schools that had proven to be much better than their small reputations would suggest.

With this very informal and unscientific survey and my notes from conversations with students and parents and some national experts, I have put together the list below of 100 schools that deserve more attention than they are getting.

This is, admittedly, a very fluid and idiosyncratic way to look at higher education. Reputations can change quickly. Schools that might have been on such a list a generation ago, like Middlebury or Wesleyan, are now recognized to be first-class institutions who have nowhere near enough room for all the students who want to get in. Many schools listed below may soon find themselves in that situation, and some are there already. Colleges like Occidental and Grinnell have become so popular I was reluctant to include them here. But the counselors and teachers know more than I do. They say these schools are underappreciated, so here they are.

I have ranked the hundred schools, but I would not put much stock in my order of merit. I did it mostly for fun. You can't lure people into a friendly argument over which school is best unless you do some ranking. I have stacked them based on how often they were mentioned by counselors and teachers. I broke ties after assessing the fervor of the comments I received from the people I surveyed.

Please be assured that all 100 colleges below are excellent and deserve to be put on your own list if they offer something that pleases you.

Anyone who writes about schools that rise above name recognition owes a debt to Loren Pope, former *New York Times* education editor and college administrator and now one of our nation's leading educational consultants and experts on college admission. His books, particularly *Looking Beyond the Ivy League* and *Colleges That Change Lives,* identify many schools that put teaching and character development ahead of public relations and high places on the *U.S. News and World Report* list. *Colleges That Change Lives* names 40 schools, many of which appeared on the lists counselors and teachers sent me. These are schools, Pope says, where "faculty and students work closely together, learning is collaborative rather than competitive, students are involved in their own education, there is much discussion of values, and there is a sense of family."

I think I can speak for Pope, and anyone else who recommends certain colleges, in saying that all such lists leave out many good schools. For instance, I think the most under-appreciated resources in American higher education are the big state universities. They all have departments that rival the Ivy League in quality, and some of them are as good as Harvard, Yale, or Princeton in every conceivable category except the ability to turn the heads of the college administrators whose subjective judgments determine the *U.S. News* list. I particularly like the fact that the big state schools have so many majors and so many extracurricular organizations that a young person experimenting with alternate career choices can switch from one field to another with relative ease, even if getting into the right courses immediately can be a struggle.

There are also many smaller schools with friendly, intelligent approaches to learning that are not mentioned below. I limited myself to 100 schools so that this chapter would not take up all the space allotted for this book. In your own journey through the world of American colleges and universities, you will find splendid schools that I have never heard of. Please give them serious consideration, and then tell me about them. My email address is mathewsj@washpost.com. I am always eager to learn about wonderful schools everyone should know about.

1. ELON UNIVERSITY

Elon, N.C.; www.elon.edu; 800-334-8448

This campus of 4,160 undergraduates gets enthusiastic reviews. Alice T. Ledford works as a college placement counselor at the American International School in Riyadh, Saudi Arabia, but she once was an administrator at Elon and thinks its standards of student service are remarkable. "It is an ideal place for students who want a supportive environment," she said. "The student services staff provides many extracurricular activities and opportunities for service learning. It is the most amazing place with regard to dealing with student crises." Sally O'Rourke, a counselor at Andover (Mass.) High School, said students who went to Elon thrived on its "emphasis on leadership, service, hands-on learning, and study abroad." Mary Ann Willis, a college counselor at Bayside Academy in Daphne, Ala., complimented Elon's "forward-looking" leadership that provides "a great setting and realistic notions about adolescents and education." She said she was particularly impressed that, unlike most schools, Elon publishes its National Survey of Student Engagement results.

Barbara Meyer, guidance content specialist at Medfield (Mass.) High School, said Elon has "as impressive a communications program as I have ever seen, with a totally renovated campus." Pam Little, director of guidance and college counseling at the Fayetteville (N.C.) Academy, remarked on its "lovely setting with several wonderful new buildings and a campus as clean as Disney World. The faculty goes the extra mile to help students and students know it."

2. EARLHAM COLLEGE

Richmond, Ind.; www.earlham.edu; 765-983-1499

This small school of slightly more than 1,000 undergraduates is on Pope's list and has many admirers. Becky Handel, a counselor at Bishop Luers High School in Fort Wayne, Ind., said the college "is Quaker founded and adheres to the beliefs of the Quaker tradition. If you have a student who is bright, has perhaps underachieved in high school, and is not afraid to walk to the beat of a different drummer, from the heart, this is a wonderful jewel." Mark Gathercole, college advisor at the Jakarta International School, said "what a sleeper—a real community of learners, prompted by its Quaker heritage." Bruce Vinik, an educational consultant and former director of college counseling at the Georgetown Day School in Washington, D.C., said "it also has a highly regarded Japanese Studies program."

3. CLARK UNIVERSITY

Worchester, Mass.; www.clarku.edu; 508-793-7711

This institution of about 1,900 undergraduates has high quality, but still admits B students. Dory Streett [cq], a high school counselor at the

American School of Milan, said Clark is "one of the few small liberal arts colleges where a truly socially diverse student body co-exists harmoniously." She said the school has "outstanding programs in geography and psychology." Sally O'Rourke, a counselor at Andover (Mass.) High School, said Clark "really looks at the individual kid" and has "great scientific research happening." In Kaplan's *Unofficial, Biased Insider's Guide to the 320 Most Interesting Colleges,* Trent Anderson says "Clark's psychology and geology programs command national respect, and its research opportunities are unheard of for such a small school."

4. COLLEGE OF WOOSTER

Wooster, Ohio; www.wooster.edu; 330-263-2000

The Presbyterian-affiliated school has 1,750 undergraduates and is known for its independent study program. The student-faculty ratio is very low, 11.5 to one. The 240-acre campus has a nine-hole golf course. Bruce Vinik, formerly director of college counseling at the Georgetown Day School, said this is "a very good liberal arts college that has a surprisingly eclectic and interesting student body. The teaching is excellent and students get a great deal of individual attention. The school has a very strong music program."

5. KALAMAZOO COLLEGE

Kalamazoo, Mich.; www.kzoo.edu; 800-253-3602

The college has an unusual "K Plan" that combines classroom study, overseas travel, internships, and a senior thesis. Dory Streett [cq], a counselor at the American School of Milan, said she was impressed that more than 85 percent of Kalamazoo students study abroad. The school also has an exceptional physics department, she said. Mark Gathercole, counselor and college advisor at the Jakarta International School, said the school is distinguished by "personal attention and great teaching." Educational consultant Bruce Vinik complimented its "internships and overseas study."

6. RHODES COLLEGE

Memphis, Tenn.; www.rhodes.edu; 901-843-3000

Also on Pope's list, the college is described by the Princeton Review's *The Best 345 Colleges* as "one of the best kept secrets in higher education." Richard James, education professor and coordinator of school counseling at the University of Memphis, described Rhodes as "a private college which costs a lot of money to go to" but "will give you a twenty megaton liberal education. Students who come out of this place can think and write." Pam Little of the Fayetteville (N.C.) Academy said the campus is beautiful and "the faculty gives its all to further intellectual development. I sat through a music appreciation class [that] was stimulating and as technically up to date as any major university."

7. GUILFORD COLLEGE

Greensboro, N.C.; www.guilford.edu; 336-316-2000

Located on a beautiful campus in central North Carolina, Guilford is distinguished by its very loose course requirements, although the faculty watches closely to make sure each student is moving toward a sound academic goal. Carol West, a college counselor at the American International School in Egypt, said "it is a favorite of mine for a solid B student or higher who is liberal arts oriented. It is a 'kind' place." Sally O'Rourke at Andover (Mass.) High said the Quaker school has a "values-based, student-centered" program with strong academics.

8. OCCIDENTAL COLLEGE

Los Angeles, Calif.; www.oxy.edu; 323-259-2500

I spent my freshman year at this school and have visited several times since. I admire its evolution into a campus deeply engaged in the southern California community. I no longer think it is underappreciated. In fact, Oxy has become very hot. But many guidance counselors still insist that it isn't getting the attention it deserves. Carl Schulkin, associate director of college counseling at Pembroke Hill School in Kansas City, Mo., said Oxy "has a very diverse student body and a faculty truly devoted to undergraduate teaching." Brian Aguilar, academic coordinator for the Upward Bound Program at the University of California–Davis, called it "a small private liberal arts college with an excellent academic reputation." In *The Unofficial, Biased Insider's Guide to the 320 Most Interesting Colleges,* Kaplan Inc. vice president of learning and assessment Seppy Basili said, "Occidental is about cultural diversity. If you can't deal with that, ask yourself why."

9. WASHINGTON COLLEGE

Chestertown, Md.; www.washcoll.edu; 800-422-1782

Under John S. Toll, former chancellor of the University of Maryland, this small school has begun to develop a national reputation and win the hearts of many high school staffers. Cathy Henderson Stein, who works in the career information center at Montgomery Blair High School in Silver Spring, Md., said the school does "a great job of getting their kids into med schools." Bob Ammann, a counselor at Kwajalein High School in the Marshall Islands, said the college "is very student oriented" and offers "$10,000 a year to members of the National Honor Society." Peggy Hanselman, a counselor at New Hope (Penn.) Solebury High School, said "it provides a solid liberal arts education by dedicated faculty and admissions staff members on an elegant and petite campus."

10. ILLINOIS WESLEYAN UNIVERSITY

Bloomington, Ill.; www.iwu.edu; 309-556-1000

An ambitious building program has helped give this school of 2,100 undergraduates a national reputation. Mary Juraska, college consultant at Marian Catholic High School in Chicago Heights, Ill., said it has "strong fine arts, liberal arts and sciences" and "an excellent success rate for students applying to medical school." Barbara Sams, a college admissions specialist at Lafayette High School in Wildwood, Mo., said it has "absolutely fabulous facilities—it's for top performing students."

11. TRINITY UNIVERSITY

San Antonio, Tex.; www.trinity.edu; 210-999-7011

This institution of 2,300 undergraduates has had success offering generous scholarships to top students, while building first-class business administration and computer science programs. Natalie Root, an International Baccalaureate teacher at Washington-Lee High School in Arlington, Va., recalled a family that had "nothing but high praise" for the school. The parents said their son "was completely besotted by the school and, the most important words to parents, they said the value for money was outstanding."

12. KENYON COLLEGE

Gambier, Ohio; www.kenyon.edu; 800-848-2468

The college has long had a reputation for intellectual quality and close faculty-student relationships. Connie Decker, counselor at John W. North High School in Riverside, Calif., said "very bright students who are not necessarily interested in the 'name game' love it." Mark Gathercole, counselor and college advisor at the Jakarta International School, said although the campus is "located in rural Ohio, its personal attention, high quality instruction, and lots of campus activities make students forget that it's not near a big metropolis."

13. WHITMAN COLLEGE

Walla Walla, Wash.; www.whitman.edu; 877-462-9448

The college of about 1,400 students has an admissions policy emphasizing essays and extracurricular activities over SATs. "The college cares much more about who you are and what you have to offer," the Princeton Review said. Dorothy Hay, a counselor at Liberty High School in the Issaquah school district east of Seattle, said students like Whitman's rural setting and a great city park "with lovely white swans." The college is strong in sciences, drama, foreign language, history, math, political science, and pre-law, she said, and is "perfect for the high achiever who doesn't have a clue what they want to do for their first career after graduation."

14. GRINNELL COLLEGE

Grinnell, Ohio; www.grinnell.edu; 641-269-4000

The college, established in 1846 by a group of transplanted New Englanders with close ties to the Congregational Church, has long committed itself to social reform. It has about 1,350 students in a rural part of the country. There are relatively few minorities, but there is a strong academic emphasis and lots of volunteer opportunities. Its Web site says "if the future of a college can be found in its past, then concern with social issues, educational innovation, and individual expression will continue to shape Grinnell."

15. WHEATON COLLEGE

Wheaton, Ill.; www.wheaton.edu; 630-752-5000

Christian moral principals are important at this campus of 2,400 undergraduates. Kaplan's unofficial biased guide said it "may truly be the Harvard of Christian higher education." Kaplan said "the scriptures are the core of the education, and biblical studies are required. Students aren't shielded from the subjects that challenge their faith, like abortion or cloning, but one student reports that a faculty member's contract wasn't renewed because of his views on evolution." Sally O'Rourke at Andover (Mass.) High praised Wheaton's strong academics and supportive community, as well as its well-conceived honor code.

16. DICKINSON COLLEGE

Carlisle, Penn.; www.dickinson.edu; 717-243-5121

The school has 2,200 undergraduates and is losing its reputation as a refuge for rich kids, with its academic standards higher than ever and opportunities for study abroad increasing. Cathy Henderson Stein, who works in the career information center at Montgomery Blair High School in Silver Spring, Md., said Dickinson has a "really great foreign language department and is good for pre-law." Cigus Vanni, a counselor facilitator at Cherry Hill High School West in New Jersey, said "my visits to Dickinson in the last couple years have been wonderful—the spirit on campus is high [and] the student body is thoughtful and more diverse."

17. CHRISTOPHER NEWPORT UNIVERSITY

Newport News, Va.; www.cnu.edu; 757-594-7000

The school, the youngest comprehensive university in Virginia, is developing a regional reputation as part of the rapid growth of the Tidewater area. Sunny Greene, recently retired as a college advisor at the Thomas Jefferson High School for Science and Technology in Fairfax County, Va., called Christopher Newport an "up and coming small state university with a caring faculty."

18. TRUMAN STATE UNIVERSITY

Kirksville, Mo.; www.truman.edu; 800-892-7792

With about 5,700 undergraduates, the university is one of a handful of tax-supported schools that have gained national reputations by focusing on small classes and high academic standards. Barbara Harris Lord, a counselor at Plattsburg (Mo.) Accelerated High School, said Truman State has an excellent teacher education department. It is known for its intimate, small-campus atmosphere, and low teacher-student ratio. Jean Peterson of Purdue University's department of educational studies said the revamped and renamed school, formerly Northeast Missouri State, has "low tuition, stellar programs, and many blue-collar, bright students from Kansas City and St. Louis."

19. WESTMINSTER COLLEGE

Fulton, Mo.; www.westminster-mo.edu; 573-642-3361

Famous as the site of Winston Churchill's "Iron Curtain" speech in 1946, the tiny school—only 700 students—has fashioned a program based on the values of integrity, fairness, respect, and responsibility. Barbara Sams, a college admissions specialist at Lafayette High School in Wildwood, Mo., said it has a particularly good record for preparing students for law and medical schools.

20. LOYOLA MARYMOUNT UNIVERSITY

Los Angeles, Calif.; www.lmu.edu; 310-338-2700

The school is one of 28 Jesuit universities in the United States. It emphasizes its close ties to the culture and economy of Southern California, and it recruits heavily in Hispanic neighborhoods. Brian Aguilar, academic coordinator of the Upward Bound Program at the University of California–Davis, said "this fine, small, private Jesuit college is often overlooked in the Los Angeles area, where UCLA and USC hold the popular mind share."

21. MACALESTER COLLEGE

St. Paul, Minn.; www.macalester.edu; 651-696-6000

The school has acquired a very favorable reputation in recent years among private schools and very competitive public high schools for possessing Ivy qualities and yet having room for more than just students with stellar SAT scores. But that in turn has made admission more competitive. Sunny Greene, former college advisor at the Thomas Jefferson High School for Science and Technology in Fairfax County, Va., praised the college's combination of an "internationally diverse student body" and "Midwestern friendliness and support."

22. HARTWICK COLLEGE

Oneonta, N.Y.; www.hartwick.edu; 607-431-4000

Howard Uhrlass, a counselor at West Genesee High School in Camillus, N.Y., called Hartwick a "strong liberal arts school with a staff that interacts closely with students." He also praised the quality of the admissions and financial aid staff. Hartwick has what it calls its J-term, where students either study abroad for the month of January, do an intensive internship, or take a class in which they spend the month delving into the subject and doing research. Suzy Hallock-Bannigan, head counselor at Woodstock (Vt.) Union High School, said "I once had an artist who had so transformed ordinary sneakers into a work of art that it defies description—she went to Hartwick, as did a champion field hockey player. They seem to like creative people a little off center."

23. GOUCHER COLLEGE

Baltimore, Md.; www.goucher.edu; 410-337-6000

I put it on the list because so many guidance counselors mentioned it, not because I have known the college's new president, Sanford J. Ungar, since we were on the same college newspaper together more than a third of a century ago. Its proximity to the many cultural attractions of Baltimore is a plus, and its strong science and writing programs have added to its reputation. Sally O'Rourke at Andover (Mass.) High said the school is very "student-centered" and has a strong arts and theater program.

24. HENDRIX COLLEGE

Conway, Ark.; www.hendrix.edu; 800-277-9017

This is one of the schools on Pope's list. The Princeton Review's *The Best 345 Colleges* said it is "an especially good bet for students with strong grades who lack the test scores usually necessary for admission to colleges on a higher level of selectivity." There are slightly over 1,000 undergraduates, making it easy for professors to get to know students. The entire campus mixes together in unusual ways. All freshmen, for instance, must take "Western Intellectual Traditions." In its region, Hendrix has the same reputation for demanding academic work in a small college as Swarthmore, Pomona, and William & Mary have nationally.

25. AUSTIN COLLEGE

Sherman, Tex.; www.austincollege.edu; 903-813-2000

Having been praised by Pope, the school has experienced a jump in applications that may soon take it off of anyone's underappreciated list. It was founded in 1849 and is affiliated with the Presbyterian Church (U.S.A.) Approximately two thirds of its students pursue advanced degrees within five years of graduating from Austin. The lakeside campus in the suburbs north of Dallas is lovely. The college offers a "January term" between the two main semesters when students are encouraged to explore a topic or a job or anything else, within reason, that suits their fancy.

26. BERRY COLLEGE

Mount Berry, Ga.; www.berry.edu; 706-232-5374

For students who do not need a bustling big city to keep them happy, this college is a rare treat. Tere Goodwin, a high school counselor in Fayette County, Ga., said Berry's "overall program is phenomenal."

Laura Herd, a teaching consultant in Greenville, S.C., who has advised students on colleges for years, said the school is "private and non-denominational but Christian in philosophy and practice." Visitors often fall in love with its location, "28,000 acres of mountains and lakes," she said. When her son visited his junior year of high school, four faculty members gave him a tour and took him to lunch, she said. Berry's isolation, said Bob Ammann, a counselor at Kwajalein High School in the Marshall Islands, makes it "among the safest colleges in the United States. Kids can jog in the middle of the night."

27. St. Olaf College

Northfield, Minn.; www.stolaf.edu; 507-646-2222

Fans of the situation comedy *The Golden Girls* may smile at the name St. Olaf, the trigger to many Betty White jokes, but there is the college in chilly Minnesota, setting a standard for academic excellence and sobriety that has won it many admirers, particularly among high school counselors. Peg Glasgow, a counselor for the Boyertown (Penn.) Area School District, called it "a jewel with a reputation that has not spread as far as its strengths warrant. It has outstanding programs in diverse areas including biology, music, and study abroad programs. They have a strong ancient studies program and excellent religion courses. There is an emphasis on understanding issues of peace, justice, and personal responsibility that permeates all levels of the school." Mark Gathercole of the Jakarta International School said "there is a great feel to it, with wonderful music, an open community and personal attention." Many members of the student body are not thrilled about the no-alcohol rule, but they seem to find many other ways to entertain themselves.

28. Bates College

Lewiston, Me.; www.bates.edu; 207-786-6255

This is another small school—about 1,800 undergraduates—with a well-earned reputation for high academic standards and easy faculty-student communication. It does not require that applicants submit SAT or ACT scores, but students who have not applied themselves to their high school courses or shown intellectual merit in some way will not get in. "My younger brother received an outstanding education there in the 1960s and it is still a fine school," said Carl Schulkin, a college counselor at Kansas City's Pembroke Hill School. "The faculty is truly devoted to undergraduate teaching."

29. ALLEGHENY COLLEGE

Meadville, Penn.; www.allegheny.edu; 814-332-3100

Allegheny has 1,900 undergraduates and a historic affiliation with the United Methodist Church. Pope said it "has a long and distinguished record of producing not only future scientists and scholars, but business leaders as well." There are more than 336 public computers scattered about the 72-acre central campus. There is also a 182-acre outdoor recreational complex, a 283-acre nature preserve, a $14.5 million science complex, and a $13 million indoor recreation center.

30. DAVIDSON COLLEGE

Davidson, N.C.; www.davidson.edu; 704-894-2000

This is another school that I would say is no longer underappreciated. It accepts only about 35 percent of applicants, making it tougher to get into than Wellesley or Carleton or any of a number of brand-name colleges. The academic demands on its 1,600 undergraduates are unusually intense, but that has only added to its reputation. Sunny Greene, former college advisor at Jefferson High in Fairfax County, Va., praised the college's "serious academics" and "respected honor code." Mary Ann Willis of Bayside Academy said "they do an extraordinary job of matching students to share rooms."

31. COLORADO COLLEGE

Colorado Springs, Colo.; www.coloradocollege.edu; 800-542-7214

Students who choose to spend their high school years in extraordinarily difficult Advanced Placement or International Baccalaureate courses are eagerly recruited by Colorado College. It has become fashionable among families that look for Ivy-like colleges. Suzy Hallock-Bannigan of Woodstock (Vt.) Union High said "Colorado is a good bet for the student who can really focus as they have a unique system in which a student studies one thing at a time and the term changes every month. They have a summer session, 90 acres a hard hour outside of Denver, and decent intimacy (2000-ish students). The kids aren't just computer numbers. This is a juicy and fun place with standards and scenery."

32. GETTYSBURG COLLEGE

Gettysburg, Penn.; www.gettysburg.edu; 717-337-6000

Many students love the charming campus in rural Pennsylvania. The student body, about 2,200 undergraduates, is academically motivated, if too wedded to the fraternity and sorority scene for some tastes. The history, political science, and business administration programs are good, as are the sciences. *The Fiske Guide to Colleges* said "the English department, home of the *Gettysburg Review*, is among the strongest" of all the college's departments.

33. QUINNIPIAC UNIVERSITY

Hamden, Conn.; www.quinnipiac.edu; 800-462-1944

The school began in 1929 as the Connecticut College of Commerce. It still has a strong commitment to preparing students for the business world, as well as the health science and communication fields. It is a liberal arts institution on a lovely campus, and one of those places rising in prominence even though it is less likely to be mentioned in the college guides.

34. MILLSAPS COLLEGE

Jackson, Miss.; www.millsaps.edu; 601-974-1000

"Jackson has a thriving arts community and Millsaps is located to take advantage of the political, business, and arts opportunities surrounding it," said Mary Ann Willis of Bayside Academy. "The size of the place lends it to smaller, more discussion-oriented classes. Scholarship money is available and internships are a plus." Its premed, music, history and English faculties are excellent and underline the notion that state capitals are a good place to look for interesting colleges. Fraternities and sororities rule the social scene.

35. BARD COLLEGE

Annandale-on-Hudson, N.Y.; www.bard.edu; 845-758-7472

The college's president, Leon Botstein, is one of the few higher education leaders anyone has ever heard of. He is a violinist, conductor, and music scholar, and an advocate for reform whose acidic sense of humor has made him a popular speaker and government advisor. The school is dedicated to academic excellence and intellectual discourse, and everyone must complete a Senior Project, either a thesis or some other original work. The isolated campus appeals to some, but not all.

36. YORK COLLEGE OF PENNSYLVANIA

York, Penn.; www.ycp.edu; 717-846-7788

Louis J. Bamonte, guidance chairperson at Walter G. O'Connell Copiague High School in Copiague, N.Y., said York "has a good selection of programs" and because of strong alumni support, tuition "is very inexpensive as far as private schools are concerned." Marilee Kessler, counselor at Central York High School, said this college in her town "does everything first class!" She said "the county has a large industrial base and students have worked at companies such as Harley Davidson. The business administration program offers a masters degree as well as undergraduate degrees in finance, administration, marketing, management, international business, and information systems. A $1 million Fine Arts Center is in the center of campus." There are also programs in nursing, criminal justice, education, and mechanical engineering.

37. MUHLENBERG COLLEGE

Allentown, Penn.; www.muhlenberg.edu; 484-664-3100

The college has aggressively promoted its no-SAT, no-ACT admissions policy, and has in the process become very selective, admitting only 35 percent of applicants. The campus is beautiful and the faculty very lively. Bruce Vinik, a Maryland-based consultant who was formerly director of college counseling at the Georgetown Day School, said Muhlenberg is "a fine liberal arts college with a strong sense of community. It does a particularly good job preparing students for medical school and also has a very good theater program."

38. KEENE STATE COLLEGE

Keene, N.H.; www.keene.edu; 603-352-1909

This is one of the state schools which, like Truman State in Missouri, have developed an intellectual reputation and caught the attention of counselors throughout their regions. Sally O'Rourke of Andover (Mass.) High said students from her community have found Keene State to be a "great campus in a small town." She said it "looks at the individual student, not the numbers" and provides "great support for learning disabilities." Suzy Hallock-Bannigan of Woodstock (Vt.) Union High said it is "one of those teacher-training places still good for the artist, musician, or thespian. . . . They have a lab school associated with the college's education program" as well as strong psychology programs. Keene, she said, is "a darling small town with hundreds of lit pumpkins around the village green on Halloween—no kidding."

39. URSINUS COLLEGE

Collegeville, Penn.; www.ursinus.edu; 610-409-3200

This college of not much more than 1,300 undergraduates has built a strong reputation for biology and chemistry courses that prepare students for medical school. Cigus Vanni, counselor facilitator at Cherry Hill High School West in New Jersey, said when he brought a group of high school students to the college "we received extraordinary personal attention, a warm welcome in admissions and a true sense of caring." Michelle L. Underwood, a counselor who attended Ursinus, said the college has a "caring, community-type atmosphere where the students really get to know one another. Students will say hello even if they do not know the person. Almost all faculty members have office hours whenever it is convenient for the student. They take a personal interest in all of their students. Many even conduct classes in their homes." She said academic opportunities are considerable, with her being published three times when she was an undergraduate. "It's a school that many people are unfortunately unaware of," she said.

40. UNIVERSITY OF PUGET SOUND

Tacoma, Wash.; www.ups.edu; 253-879-3100

Tacoma, like nearby Seattle, is rainy, but that has not affected the warm feelings many counselors have for this school. Connie Decker at John W. North High in Riverside, Calif., said UPS is "really nurturing, individual attention abounds—lots of opportunities for students to become involved." Dorothy Hay at Liberty High in Issaquah, Wash., said its strengths are choral music, biology, English, chemistry, pre-law, pre-med, and business. She said it is a "smaller school where students have a chance to participate in activities and have caring instructors."

41. SPELMAN COLLEGE

Atlanta, Ga.; www.spelman.edu; 404-681-3643

This historically black women's college is another place mentioned by guidance counselors that I think no longer belongs on any under-appreciated list. It has a national reputation and a sense of tradition that few schools ever hope to achieve. "There is great mentoring here and the best of their students could have, in many cases, gone to an Ivy League school," said Mary Ann Willis, of Bayside Academy in Daphne, Ala. "You have the rich and famous next to the scratch-your-head-how-did-they-get-here kids and the bonds between them are tight. It is a place where both groups can and do succeed."

42. ST. LAWRENCE UNIVERSITY

Canton, N.Y.; www.stlawu.edu; 315-229-5011

St. Lawrence, with about 2,000 students, is one of many schools on this list that has created a vibrant liberal arts tradition with excellent faculty and good character values, but cannot get the attention it deserves because it is in such a remote location. The Princeton Review said this makes it "an especially good choice for academically sound but average students who are seeking an excellent small college experience and/or an outdoorsy setting."

43. ST. JOHN'S COLLEGE

Annapolis, Md., and Santa Fe, N.M.; www.sjca.edu and www.sjcsf.edu; 800-727-9238 and 505-984-6000

Here are the ultimate intellectual experiences—two schools on two lovely campuses at opposite ends of the country, joined by their commitment to the most ancient traditions of higher education. The students read the Great Books. The tutors guide their discussions. There is nothing else like them in America. The experience attracts very special students, and you have to be very sure you are one of them.

44. SAVANNAH COLLEGE OF ART AND DESIGN

Savannah, Ga.; www.scad.edu; 912-525-5100

The school has 5,500 students engaged in a range of artistic pursuits, from architecture to jewelry to video and film. Its allure is enhanced by its location in one of the loveliest and most intriguing old Southern cities. Ten percent of the students come from abroad, drawn by the rich blend of courses and the chance to get in on the campus tradition of helping all the filmmakers who find Savannah a perfect place for location shots. Films shot there include *Forrest Gump, The Legend of Bagger Vance,* and, of course, the cinematic ode to Savannah, *Midnight in the Garden of Good and Evil.*

45. WABASH COLLEGE

Crawfordsville, Ind.; www.wabash.edu; 800-345-5385

One of the last bastions of single-sex education for men, Wabash extols its "Gentleman's Rule", a promise to behave as a gentleman and responsible citizen on and off campus. It seems to work. Like the women's colleges in the 21st century, applicants are very much self-selected, and the rejection rates are not so high. But the academic demands require energy and attention. Becky Handel at Bishop Luers High in Fort Wayne, Ind., said many of her school's best students go to this liberal arts school. She called it "a small, male-only school in a small town that lives by the old code of ethics for men: Christian character and ethics are extremely important."

46. UNIVERSITY OF TAMPA

Tampa, Fla.; www.utampa.edu; 813-253-6211

This is one of the schools that I was surprised to find on the list. The private university of 3,200 undergraduates has only the beginnings of a strong regional reputation, but counselors like what they have been hearing from students. There is a $110 million building program underway. Shelly Hollingsworth, counselor of the year in Tampa's school district for her work at Tampa Bay Technical High School, said this small, local institution has an "unbelievable new business building and a rapidly growing arts program." Most of the residence halls are five years old or less.

47. HOPE COLLEGE

Holland, Mich.; www.hope.edu; 616-337-7166

The school has 3,000 undergraduates enrolled in a liberal arts program buttressed with an emphasis on Christian values. Sarah Bast, a school counselor in Knoxville, Tenn., and a Hope graduate, complimented the school's strong pre-med and pre-engineering programs. "There seems to be a lot of opportunity for students to do research with professors in a variety of disciplines, not just the sciences," she said.

48. EVERGREEN STATE COLLEGE

Olympia, Wash.; www.evergreen.edu; 360-866-6000

In keeping with the individualistic traditions of the Pacific Northwest, the 4,000 undergraduates are required to create their own course of study on this lovely campus. Dorothy Hay, a counselor at Liberty High School in Issaquah, near Seattle, said Evergreen State is famous for its refusal to give standard grades. "Instead instructors and the students evaluate the students' progress in learning, how they have mastered the subject, how they have helped others in the class to master the subject, how they have applied what they have learned to real world settings." She said "students design their own degree program based upon what they want to do after they graduate. Internships are an integral part of the program."

49. CENTRE COLLEGE

Danville, Ken.; www.centre.edu; 800-423-6236

The college of 1,000 students is considered one of the premier intellectual gathering points in its region. It draws undergraduates who were very successful in their high school courses and professors trained at many of the brand name schools. Pope put it on his list of 40. He said "profs who've been at the most famous universities said they've never experienced the kind of collegiality they enjoy at Centre."

50. MARY WASHINGTON COLLEGE

Fredericksburg, Va.; www.mwc.edu; 540-654-1000

Its strong academic reputation and low price tag as a state school have made Mary Washington a rising star. Natalie Root, a teacher at Washington-Lee High School in Arlington, Va., said "parents, former students, and other teachers I have spoken to about this school all have the same basic response, 'What a great place!' . . . The admissions office is assertively recruiting high school students who are taking the most challenging courses offered." This includes Root's daughter, who vowed never to go to a school in her home state but decided to apply early decision to Mary Washington after one visit. Root said the campus has a classic East Coast beauty and the technological facilities and bookstore are exceptional. "This school's entire mission is the undergraduate student," she said. "The faculty who actually teach in the class is close to 100 percent. The support services are fantastic. They have worked very hard to keep it from being a suitcase school where students leave each weekend. They have lots of clubs to join and programs to immerse yourself in and no frats or sororities."

51. BELOIT COLLEGE

Beloit, Wis.; www.beloit.edu; 608-363-2000

The town isn't much, but the campus of about 1,300 undergraduates has unusually good food, small classes, and an innovative faculty that have given it a solid reputation. Dory Streett [cq] of the American School of Milan said it has an "exceptional anthropology department and very good fine arts department." Keith Cincotta, counselor at the American School Dubai in the United Arab Emirates, said Beloit is a "liberal arts college that provides all kinds of opportunities for kids to become actively involved in their own education—seminars for freshmen, design your own major, an intellectually charged environment, plenty of opportunities to work with faculty members." Cincotta said "I've sent two kids there in the last few years and they both love it. Thoughtful kids who weren't necessarily activists, they both are exploring all kinds of new areas at Beloit."

52. BUCKNELL UNIVERSITY

Lewisburg, Penn.; www.bucknell.edu; 570-577-2000

The university has about 3,500 undergraduates and a solid reputation for preparing students for business, engineering, and science. Mary Ann Willis, of Bayside Academy in Daphne, Ala., summed up Bucknell this way: "Sleepy town, beautiful campus, first rate teachers, good athletics, engineers have to learn how to write and think in a liberal arts way." She said "somebody loves them because there is money for the arts at this school too."

53. DEPAUW UNIVERSITY

Greencastle, Ind.; www.depauw.edu; 800-447-2495

The beautiful campus and long tradition of excellence draw families to the school. It has a Winter Term, a month between semesters for students to get experience they can't get in the classroom. Karen Elijah, a school counselor and parent in Indiana, said Depauw is "definitely not cheap" but has an "excellent music program which can include overseas traveling, and there are scholarships available."

54. FLAGLER COLLEGE

St. Augustine, Fla.; www.flagler.edu; 904-829-6481

This is another school whose reputation is rising rapidly. Tracy L. Weaver, a guidance counselor at Fair Haven (Vt.) Union High School, said she often recommends Flagler to her students, and not just because it is her alma mater. "The classes are small, the campus is a historical landmark (the former Ponce de Leon Hotel), and the cost per year including tuition and room and board is around $10,000," she said. Mary Ann Willis, of Bayside Academy in Daphne, Ala., calls the campus "drop dead gorgeous" and that is only the beginning. "The dining hall has real Tiffany windows," she said. "The food still tastes like college food, but what a setting. They require all students to work with career planning and placement from the freshman year on. They tolerate no drugs or alcohol—students are dismissed. Also, guys aren't allowed in a girl's room and vice versa."

55. ITHACA COLLEGE

Ithaca, N.Y.; www.ithaca.edu; 800-429-4274

Overshadowed by sharing the same town with Ivy giant Cornell University, Ithaca is gaining a reputation for excellent programs in music, theater, communication, and physical therapy. It has about 6,100 undergraduates, only about half of whom are from New York. The town's status as a mecca for college students, with good bars and restaurants, is a lure for some, and Lake Cayuga provides lots of recreational opportunities and romantic vistas.

56. JOHNSON & WALES UNIVERSITY

Providence, R.I.; www.jwu.edu; 401-598-1000

Here is a school with a very well defined goal—to prepare students for careers in business, technology, or culinary arts. It was established in Providence in 1914, but now has campuses in Denver, Norfolk, Charleston, S.C., and North Miami, Fla., as well as opportunity for study in Goteborg, Sweden. Shelly Hollingsworth at Tampa Bay Technical High School said the school has a "terrific hands-on curriculum and unique financial aid packages."

57. NAZARETH COLLEGE OF ROCHESTER

Rochester, N.Y.; www.naz.edu; 716-586-2525

The institution was founded by the Sisters of St. Joseph, Nazareth, in 1924, but has been an independent private college for more than 30 years. It has about 1,600 full time undergraduates, but is in the midst of a major expansion, including the purchase of a 73-acre tract next door, that will raise enrollment to about 2,000 in 2005. It has strong programs in education, health and social work, and a long string of students successful in winning Fulbright scholarships abroad. Mike Stahl of Schenectady High School said the liberal arts college has a "warm and friendly atmosphere, and some great majors in education, speech and hearing, and physical training."

58. WESTERN CAROLINA UNIVERSITY

Cullowhee, N.C.; www.wcu.edu; 877-928-4968

Counselors have remarked on the 265-acre campus, nestled between the Great Smoky and Blue Ridge Mountains. Annual expenses are about $6,500 for in-state students and $15,500 for out of state. It was the first university in the North Carolina system to require all students to own their own computers. It has an Honors College and a wide range of majors.

59. University of Redlands

Redlands, Calif.; www.redlands.edu; 909-335-4074

The 2,000-undergraduate, private school has long had a good reputation in California, and that is spreading. Students may design their
own majors. The classes are small. The campus covers 140-acres in a
lovely, hilly suburban community, close to Interstate 10 and all the
pleasant distractions of Southern California. It is a liberal arts school
that competes, both for applicants and in athletics, with other small
private schools, including Occidental and the Claremont colleges.

60. Paul Smith's College

Paul Smiths [cq], N.Y.; www.paulsmiths.edu; 800-421-2605

I suspect guidance counselors recommend this college, at least in
part, because they want an excuse to visit a place that looks much
more like a mountain resort than an institution of higher learning.
Paul Smith's (no one has explained to me why the school gets an
apostrophe and the town doesn't) began as an Adirondacks vacation
stop, Paul Smith's Hotel, which attracted Teddy Roosevelt, Grover
Cleveland, Irving Berlin, and Henry Ford. It now offers degrees in biology and natural resources as well as business, travel and tourism,
and culinary arts and service management. Mike Stahl, a counselor at
Schenectady (N.Y.) High School, said the college, with both two-year
and four-year degrees, is "wonderful for the outdoor enthusiast." He
said the school has a "great culinary program, lots of individual support, a very attentive faculty and great mountain scenery."

61. Saint Louis University

St. Louis, Mo.; www.slu.edu; 314-977-2222

The Jesuit university emphasizes career programs, as well as solid
academic work. Mary Juraska at Marian Catholic High in Chicago
Heights said the school of 7,200 undergraduates is "highly regarded

by Illinois counselors, especially for physical therapy, business, and accounting." Mary Ann Willis, of Bayside Academy in Daphne, Ala., was impressed by the Micah House Program—"an extraordinary social action experience for students." Campus housing has improved considerably and "you can walk to the St. Louis Shakespeare Company from campus and you can see the Fox Theatre down the street from the front of the admissions building," Willis said.

62. SANTA CLARA UNIVERSITY

Santa Clara, Calif.; www.scu.edu; 408-554-4700

Brian Aguilar, academic coordinator of the Upward Board Program at UC–Davis, said this private college in Silicon Valley has "an excellent pre-med reputation." The undergraduate program includes liberal arts, business and engineering. The school has 4,300 undergraduates and an affiliation with the Roman Catholic church, but students tell the Princeton Review that the campus is not particularly religious. Its Bay Area location is, for many applicants, a huge plus.

63. WESTERN NEW ENGLAND COLLEGE

Springfield, Mass.; www.wnec.edu; 800-325-1122

The college of 2,000 undergraduates on a lovely campus in western Massachusetts began in 1919 as a few college courses at the Springfield Central YMCA. It now offers a broad range of majors in the arts and sciences, plus business and engineering, and part-time programs at 20 locations throughout the state.

64. UNIVERSITY OF TULSA

Tulsa, Okla.; www.utulsa.edu; 918-631-2307

The oldest private university in Oklahoma, TU was founded in Muskogee as the Presbyterian School for Indian Girls. It now has

2,769 undergraduates of every ethnic background and a student/ faculty ratio of 11 to one. The strong science program is augmented by well-organized opportunities for undergraduate research. Barbara Sams, a college admissions specialist at Lafayette High in Wild-wood, Mo., said it has very strong programs in business and computer science.

65. LEWIS & CLARK COLLEGE

Portland, Ore.; www.lclark.edu; 503-768-7188

Portland has become one of the great college towns, and Lewis & Clark students enjoy the ambiance. There are about 1,700 undergraduates on a campus with a long tradition of liberal political activism and popular majors in psychology, English, and biology. Mark Gathercole at the Jakarta International School said his students rave about the personal attention they get. "Professors actually know their kids' names," he said. "There is real awareness of international students and international affairs."

66. MANHATTANVILLE COLLEGE

Purchase, N.Y.; www.mville.edu; 914-694-2200

The beautiful 100-acre campus in Westchester County has 1,400 undergraduates pursuing liberal arts studies, with a strong emphasis on training teachers and providing internships with a variety of businesses.

67. WILLAMETTE UNIVERSITY

Salem, Ore.; www.willamette.edu; 503-370-6303

State capitals often have attractive colleges and universities, and Salem is no exception. Willamette's political science program benefits from its proximity to Oregon's seat of government and an internship program in Washington, D.C. Willamette has about 1,800 undergraduates. The dorms are nice, the students nicer, and the school's strong liberal arts tradition has made it a regional favorite.

68. TEXAS CHRISTIAN UNIVERSITY

Fort Worth, Tex.; www.tcu.edu; 817-257-7000

This was another guidance counselor recommendation that surprised me. I thought of TCU as a big sports school with very strong fraternities and sororities, and it is that. But high school staffers say it also has excellent programs in business, journalism, health science, and education, and a beautiful campus.

69. BIRMINGHAM-SOUTHERN COLLEGE

Birmingham, Ala.; www.bsc.edu; 205-226-4600

It calls itself "Southern Ivy." Mary Ann Willis, college counselor at Bayside Academy in Daphne, Ala., said "the president knows the students by name and remembers them for years. They have strong pre-professional programs and solid support for the arts. Their GALA program recognizing outstanding women draws the big names as recipients." There are 1,400 undergraduates, many drawn to the well-regarded business administration courses.

70. COLLEGE OF ST. SCHOLASTICA

Duluth, Minn.; www.css.edu; 800-447-5444

Linnea Velsvaag, a guidance counselor in Minnesota, said the four-year college "has the best anatomy & physiology (cadaver lab) I know of in the state. The chemistry department is incredible also. I tell my would-be medical/nursing students to at least go to St. Scholastica for their first two years to take advantage of the fabulous science department."

71. UNIVERSITY OF THE PACIFIC

Stockton, Calif.; www.uop.edu; 800-959-2867

The university has about 3,200 undergraduates on a lovely campus close enough—if you have a car—for regular visits to San Francisco and Sacramento or the Sierra Nevada mountains. "This is one of the most beautiful campuses I've ever seen, modeled after Yale's campus," said Lori Patton, a counselor at Casa Roble Fundamental High School in Orangevale, Calif. "This is a pricier college; however, you get what you pay for. Once you begin your search into this college, you begin to feel at home and immediately see yourself as part of the family. This college is generous with scholarships and financial aid and will provide an academic haven that will last a lifetime. The professors call absentee students to check on their welfare, and they also attend graduation ceremonies and private family parties."

72. LAWRENCE UNIVERSITY

Appleton, Wis.; www.lawrence.edu; 800-227-0982

The school has only about 1,350 undergraduates who say the campus is socially slow but comfortable, and full of academic challenges. Andrew McNeill, director of college counseling at the Taft School in Watertown, Conn., called Lawrence "long on intellectualism and diversity of thinking." He said the school has made great strides in recruiting minority students and "the faculty there is tremendous. Were it not in Wisconsin, it would be very selective."

73. AGNES SCOTT COLLEGE

Decatur, Ga.; www.agnesscott.edu; 800-868-8602

This is one of the smallest schools on this list, and one of the few that admits only women. There are less than 900 undergraduates, who gravitate toward a tradition of liberal arts in a southern atmosphere with a strong connection between faculty and students. It also has one of the largest portions of African American students of any non-historically black school on this list—23 percent.

74. BEREA COLLEGE

Berea, Ken.; www.berea.edu; 859-985-3000 x3500

This Appalachian college was founded in 1855 by John G. Fee, an ardent abolitionist. It was dedicated from its beginning to inter-racial education and to the betterment of the poverty-stricken region. It pioneered a work program so that poor students could afford a private liberal arts education. Today, 80 percent of its students come from Kentucky and the Appalachian region. Its agriculture and natural resources department explores ways to make small farming more productive and less damaging to the environment. Barbara Y. Willis, a professional counselor in Nashville, said the college "has been outstanding in recruiting minority students." She said Berea has even developed a program for female students who have children.

75. AUGUSTANA COLLEGE

Sioux Falls, S.D.; www.augie.edu; 605-274-0770

The 100-acre campus is affiliated with the Evangelical Lutheran Church in America and has about 1,650 undergraduates. In recent years nearly $20 million has been invested in new centers for social science, western studies, and humanities. A Center for Visual Arts is planned. Jan Larson, a counselor at Worthington (Minn.) High School, said Augustana is "a relatively small liberal arts college with terrific programs in music, teacher education, and nursing, among others." Jean Peterson of Purdue's educational studies department praised its "fine, fine faculty."

76. Bowling Green State University

Bowling Green, Ohio; www.bgsu.edu; 419-372-2531

From its beginnings as a teacher-training college, Bowling Green has grown into a major institution with 260 different major degree programs and more than 16,000 undergraduates. About 65 percent of students receive financial aid. There are 30 instructional microcomputer laboratories across campus and a computer lab in every residence complex. Karen Elijah, a school counselor in Indiana, praised the school's "gorgeous, well-kept campus."

77. Adelphi University

Garden City, N.Y.; www.adelphi.edu; 516-877-3000

Adelphi was founded in 1896, the first co-educational college in New York state. The emphasis in on liberal arts, as well as pre-professional programs in medicine, law, business, government, scientific research, and media. An Honors College recruits advanced students interested in interdisciplinary work. Anita R. Vogel, director of guidance and careers for the East Islip (N.Y.) school district, said at Adelphi, "students get a lot of personal attention. Science labs and dorms were refurbished about two years ago and a new dorm is being built." She said it also has a good theater program.

78. University of Denver

Denver, Colo.; www.du.edu; 303-871-2036

This campus in a large and vibrant city has attracted many students with business careers in mind, but it is also working to strengthen its liberal arts courses. There are 3,900 undergraduates. Mary Ann Willis, of Bayside Academy in Daphne, Ala., said "they are bucking a trend—many schools are eliminating interviews as part of the admission process, while they have gone back to them. They are very business and tech savvy, wired in a good way."

79. HOBART & WILLIAM SMITH COLLEGES

Geneva, N.Y.; www.hws.edu; 315-781-3000

These schools, a men's college and a women's college joined together, have 1,900 undergraduates on a verdant campus alongside Seneca Lake. There are small classes and a strong commitment to a liberal arts education for all. "We have sent some students there that other colleges may have thought lop-sided," said Suzy Hallock-Bannigan, director of counseling services at Woodstock (Vt.) Union High School. "But HWS thought them gifted in one way or another. One was an athlete with an alcoholic mom, another was a born-again Christian, and the college did equally well with disparate folks like these. They come up with remarkable funding opportunities and they seem to have that old Avis we-try-harder attitude."

80. UNIVERSITY OF THE SOUTH

Sewanee, Tenn.; www.sewanee.edu; 931-598-1238

This school has long been popular among academically ambitious students in its region. "Students and families either instantly love this place or automatically rule its remote location out," said Mary Ann Willis, college counselor at Bayside Academy in Daphne, Ala. "The campus is lovingly referred to as The Mountain. Some parents when viewing the cloistered location feel an automatic sense of safety for their students because of the remoteness." Willis praised the school's architectural integrity and financial aid program, but said its greatest strength was a deep tradition of academic excellence. Students, even freshmen, may earn gowns, treasured hand-me-downs from previous classes, based on intellectual performance. Professors invite students to dinner. Students planning for law or medical school are well served, but there is also an excellent geology-earth science program.

Those looking for action volunteer for the fire department-paramedic program.

81. Xavier University of Louisiana

New Orleans, La.; www.xula.edu; 504-483-7388

This is one of the premier historically black universities in the country and the only one that is Catholic. It has an impressive list of professional alumni. There are about 3,500 undergraduates, and one of the strongest health science programs anywhere. "It has produced a ton of doctors and pharmacists, and has great summer programs for high school students, especially in sciences, math, and computers," said Mary Ann Willis of Bayside Academy.

82. St. Andrews Presbyterian University

Laurinburg, N.C.; www.sapc.edu; 910-277-5000

"These people are alchemists," said Suzy Hallock-Bannigan of Woodstock (Vt.) Union High School. "It seems they develop students to the max and love them forever. It's a small and intimate sort of place." Alice T. Ledford of the American International School in Riyadh called St. Andrews "a jewel hidden away in southern North Carolina." She said "it is a four-year liberal arts school that is a cozy environment. Strong students will find that they can develop meaningful relationships with their Ph.D. professors and learn in more of a graduate school method than an undergraduate. Because class sizes are small, there are many opportunities to learn directly from experts instead of grad students."

83. Saint Joseph's College of Maine

Standish, Me.; www.sjcme.edu; 800-338-7057

This is a very small, co-educational college of 870 undergraduates, with plans to grow to 1,020 by 2004. It was founded in 1912 by the Sisters of Mercy and occupies 331 beautifully forested acres along the shore of Sebago Lake, 18 miles northwest of Portland. It focuses on liberal arts and sciences, education, nursing, and business, with a very active service learning program.

84. SEATTLE PACIFIC UNIVERSITY

Seattle, Wash.; www.spu.edu; 206-281-2000

This is a private university with about 2,800 undergraduates. It is located on 45 acres in the fashionable Queen Anne Hill area of Seattle and is very serious about its evangelical Christian orientation. Ruth Bigback, a counselor at Pacific Middle School in Vancouver, Wash., praised Seattle Pacific's "high standards, both academically and ethically." She said the university is "obviously committed to its students, and small enough to be able to offer the personal touch. We have found them to be gracious and helpful with every need and question. The financial aid department is approachable and works hard to assist students. It is a Christian college which excels in the arts, sciences, and professional preparation."

85. WESTERN WASHINGTON UNIVERSITY

Bellingham, Wash.; www.wwu.edu; 360-650-3000

Western, as it is called, was rated one of 31 universities nationally for a high level of individual academic attention to students by the *Kaplan/Newsweek College Catalog*. Dorothy Hay, a counselor at Liberty High School in Issaquah, Wash., said the school is at a scenic spot on the coast and specializes in international studies, orchestral music, foreign languages, art, education, English, geography, pre-law, and sociology.

86. ECKERD COLLEGE

St. Petersburg, Fla.; www.eckerd.edu; 800-456-9009

The college has about 1,600 undergraduates, many of them marine biology majors making use of the school's splendid science faculty and convenient location on Florida's Gulf Coast. *The Fiske Guide to Colleges* praised the Academy of Senior Professionals, a group that mentors Eckerd students. There are no fraternities and sororities, and the administration has been cracking down on alcohol, so students often decamp to the beach or to local bars. Applications are going up, a sign that Eckerd may be much less underappreciated in the future.

87. DREW UNIVERSITY

Madison, N.J.; www.drew.edu; 973-408-3000

The 1,500 undergraduates are drawn to a number of internships and special programs that take advantage of the campus's proximity to New York City. Students interested in Wall Street or art or international affairs have much to choose from. Since a Drew admissions director many years ago extended a merit scholarship to a student who just missed the grade point cut-off, said Cigus Vanni, a counselor facilitator at Cherry Hill High School West in New Jersey, "all my interactions with Drew have been positive, affirming and sincere. My students who have attended Drew have all loved it for the nurturance, the personal attention, and the scholastic discourse that it provides."

88. CHAPMAN UNIVERSITY

Orange, Calif.; www.chapman.edu; 714-997-6711

Chapman has 3,141 undergraduates on its campus in the middle of Orange County. Connie Decker at John W. North High in Riverside, Calif., said "this is a tier one school, in my estimation, in music, film/TV, and economics. This school has gone from safety status to far more selective and still maintained its nurturing attitude. Many students get great financial support from the school, whose donors seem to be consistently generous. State of the art new dorms, a law school, beautiful facilities; I'm really impressed by this one."

89. ALFRED UNIVERSITY

Alfred, N.Y.; www.alfred.edu; 607-871-2111

The school, with 2,100 undergraduates, is known for its majors in ceramic sciences and engineering, fine arts, and business administration. Cigus Vanni, a counselor facilitator at Cherry Hill High School West in New Jersey, joked that Alfred is so isolated in upstate New York that its zip code is E-I-E-I-O. But, he said, it has great departments in visual arts, and dance and provides a "tremendous amount of personal attention . . . in an atmosphere that welcomes differences and celebrates the artistic uniqueness that students bring to campus."

90. CARROLL COLLEGE

Helena, Mont.; www.carroll.edu; 406-447-4300

This independent Catholic liberal arts college is spread over 64 acres on a tree-covered hill in Montana's state capital. Many students are drawn to the recreational opportunities, which include hiking, mountain biking, camping, fishing, and skiing. Monica Kittock-Sargent at Farmington (Minn.) High School said the college "has a strong science program and they have consistently had a high percentage of pre-med students get into medical schools around the country."

91. LOYOLA COLLEGE IN MARYLAND

Baltimore, Md.; www.loyola.edu; 410-617-2252

This school north of downtown Baltimore has about 3,500 undergraduates who thrive in an urban environment with shops, restaurants, bars, symphonies, and big league teams in both football and baseball. The tough core curriculum weeds out those who don't understand what it means to be educated by Jesuits. "Every student I have sent there has loved it and flourished," said R. J. Hawley of the American School in Switzerland.

92. KNOX COLLEGE

Galesburg, Ill.; www.knox.edu; 800-678-5669

Several generations back, my branch of the Mathews family settled in this very rural part of Illinois. My immediate ancestors, bored out of their skulls, headed for California, but I am still fond of the area and am pleased that Knox college is recognized by counselors as a good place for students ready to work hard. The 1,200 undergraduates include many students from the Chicago area who appreciate the school's high academic standards. Many future teachers study here, and the school motto, "Freedom to Flourish," is taken seriously.

93. MIAMI UNIVERSITY

Oxford, Ohio; www.miami.muohio.edu; 513-529-1809

This is a very big state school, with more than 15,000 undergraduates. But it has built a reputation for very high academic standards and very involved faculty. Andrew McNeill, director of college counseling at the Taft School in Watertown, Conn., said of the school, "you'll never, ever meet an alum who does not love the place and speak of it with flowing praise. The place just has something great going on." *The Unofficial, Biased Insider's Guide to the 320 Most Interesting Colleges* by Kaplan says "Miami consistently ranks among the top 10 universities in the nation for the number of students studying abroad."

94. SAMFORD UNIVERSITY

Birmingham, Ala.; www.samford.edu; 205-726-3673

Samford, with about 2,900 undergraduates, offers a range of opportunities in education, nursing, pharmacy, the performing arts, and pre-professional courses for future doctors and lawyers. "This school is nestled in a nice area of Birmingham on top of a hill overlooking Lakeshore Drive," said Mary Ann Willis of Bayside Academy in Daphne, Ala. "It has sound academics, a no-nonsense approach to campus life, strong pre-professional programs integrated with good sports (baseball is a consistent winner here), small size, and attention to detail."

95. UNIVERSITY OF SCRANTON

Scranton, Penn.; matrix.scranton.edu; 570-941-7540

This Jesuit school has 3,500 full-time undergraduates. Kenneth G. McCurdy, Scranton alumnus and director of the graduate program in counselor education at Malone College in Canton, Ohio, said the university is distinguished by "small class sizes, high academic expectations, close community environment, a metropolis campus that maintains a community atmosphere, and faculty and staff that are actively involved with the student body." Barbara Meyer at Medfield (Mass.) High School said it is "not the most beautiful, but every kid I ever sent there has been happy."

96. RANDOLPH-MACON COLLEGE

Ashland, Va.; www.rmc.edu; 804-752-7305

This co-educational college of 1,150 undergraduates wins praise from counselors for close attention to students and small classes. The campus is lovely. Relations between students are close, and the library and computer facilities are exceptional. About 60 percent of graduates go on to professional or graduate schools within five years.

97. SIENA COLLEGE

Londonville, N.Y.; www.siena.edu; 518-783-2300

The school has about 3,000 undergraduates and a strong history department, as well as popular business majors. Mike Stahl at Schenectady (N.Y.) High complimented the college's "outstanding admission staff" for being "extremely supportive and helpful." He said the school has a "caring atmosphere with strong academic programs." Anita R.

Vogel of the East Islip (N.Y.) school district noted that the college gives students a great deal of personal attention and has a strong community service focus. There is also, she said, a new science building.

98. LAMBUTH UNIVERSITY

Jackson, Tenn.; www.lambuth.edu; 800-526-2884

This United Methodist Church-related school in West Tennessee has a liberal arts tradition with small classes and a fine campus. Students are required to take two courses in religion, but guidance counselors say the church influence is not oppressive. "It turns out students who can read, write, and think," said Richard James, education professor and coordinator of school counseling at the University of Memphis. "They are also not an outrageous private school as far as cost is concerned."

99. OHIO UNIVERSITY

Athens, Ohio; www.ohiou.edu; 740-593-1000

About to celebrate its bicentennial in 2004, this is the oldest public institution of higher learning in Ohio and a favorite of college guides that look for best buys. It has nearly 17,000 undergraduates and a strong academic standing that makes it attractive even to out-of-state applicants. "Definitely a gem," said Mary Juraska, college consultant with Marian Catholic High School in Chicago Heights, Ill, "And it has a great communications program."

100. DEAN COLLEGE

Franklin, Mass.; www.dean.edu; 877-879-3326

The school is in the midst of making the transition from two-year to four-year school, with a bachelor's degree in dance and a collaboration with Suffolk University to offer other full degrees. It has unusual links to the mutual fund industry and a warmth and accessibility that has impressed some counselors.

INDEX

ABOUT THE AUTHOR

Jay Mathews is an education reporter and columnist for the *Washington Post,* where he has been a local, national, foreign, and business correspondent for 32 years.

Mathews was born in Long Beach, Calif., in 1945 and grew up in San Mateo, Calif., where he attended Hillsdale High School. After studying government and Chinese and working on the student newspaper at Harvard, he served with the U.S. Army in Vietnam and then returned to Harvard for a master's degree in East Asian regional studies.

He joined the *Post* as a local reporter in 1971, and in 1976 he became the *Post* bureau chief in Hong Kong. From 1981 to 1992 Mathews was the *Post* bureau chief in Los Angeles, where he wrote two books, *Escalante: The Best Teacher in America* and *A Mother's Touch.* He won the National Education Reporting Award in 1984 for a series on job retraining for automobile workers.

Mathews' fourth book, *Class Struggle: What's Wrong (and Right) with America's Best Public High Schools,* was published by Times Books in 1998. It was the first detailed look at the dynamics of elite public high schools. Excerpted in *Newsweek,* it ranked the nation's most challenging schools and revealed how schools denied many students a chance to take their most demanding courses. His rating system for high schools, the Challenge Index, is used by *Newsweek* and several other news organizations and school districts.

His column, "Class Struggle," now appears each Tuesday on the *Post's* Web site: www.washingtonpost.com. He won the 1999 Benjamin Fine Award for Outstanding Education Reporting for both feature writing and column writing.

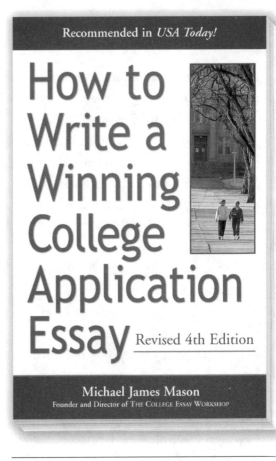